THE PROGRESSIVE ERA

AMERICAN PROBLEM STUDIES

Under the editorial direction of
OSCAR HANDLIN

The Causes of the War of 1812—BRADFORD PERKINS
Jacksonian Democracy—JAMES L. BUGG, JR.
The Mexican War—RAMÓN E. RUIZ
The Progressive Era—ARTHUR MANN
The New Deal—MORTON KELLER

THE
PROGRESSIVE ERA
Liberal Renaissance or Liberal Failure?

Edited by ARTHUR MANN

Smith College

HOLT, RINEHART AND WINSTON
New York • Chicago • San Francisco • Toronto • London

Cover photos of Theodore Roosevelt
and Woodrow Wilson courtesy of
Bettmann Archives

CONTENTS

CONTENTS

INTRODUCTION

The Progressive era is a chapter in the history of early twentieth-century American liberalism. Opinions differ over why it began and ended, what it stood for, whether it changed American life for the good, and how it is related to Populism and the New Deal. The disagreement underlying all others is whether Progressivism was modern enough for the century in which it was born. This book of readings is about that debate.

To at least this much there is general assent. The foundations of the society we live in today were created between 1880 and 1920 by industrialization, urbanization, and immigration. Those forty years were America's "take-off point" into modernity, and the blessings of course have been prodigious. But like every nation before or since, the United States paid a high price for the new in social dislocation, moral confusion, and human suffering. There was fantastic progress but abysmal poverty, one writer observed of the early stages in the process. The response to this and other paradoxes deriving from the rapid transformation of a commercial-agricultural civilization was the Progressive movement.

The most obvious paradox was the maldistribution of wealth, power, and prestige in a country that boasted equalitarian traditions. It explains why men of good will were agitated by the slum problem and the farm problem, the Negro problem and the immigrant problem, the trust problem and the labor problem, and the problem of the political machine. Could the open society, whose values descended from an earlier and less complicated time, survive in the twentieth century? That question was on the mind of Frederick Jackson Turner, the celebrated historian of agrarian America, when he noted that the New World was in danger of succumbing to the social diseases of the Old.

Historians have recently rediscovered a pre-Progressive generation in the 1880s and 1890s that anticipated the Progressives of 1900–1920 in their idealism, social criticism, ultimate objectives, and even in some of their specific demands. A minority in the population, these first reformers won some legislative victories, but they were far more important in awakening the democratic conscience. By the twentieth century, for example, three million copies had been sold of Henry George's *Progress and Poverty* (1879) and Edward Bellamy's *Looking Backward* (1888). It mattered little that George converted only a handful of people to the single tax and that Bellamy attracted even less to socialism. The two writers made the best-seller lists of their day because their appeal was appropriate to the times. Something must be done, they were saying, to solve The Social Question.

By the 1910s an active consensus for reform defined the goals in nearly every area of American life. That decade was the high noon of the Progressive era. In the 1912 Presidential election—to cite the most obvious illustration— the Democratic Wilson, the Progressive (party) Roosevelt, the Socialist Debs, and even the Republican Taft stood to the left of every President between the Civil War and 1900. The same was true, and had been true for a decade and more, of many political leaders in the cities and the states. Americans other than politicians moved left between 1900 and World War I: businessmen and trade unionists; women as well as men; Protestant, Jewish, and Catholic clergymen; writers, artists, scholars, publishers, social workers, lawyers; above all, the electorate.

What textbooks call *the* Progressive movement was actually several movements. The reader should keep that in mind, for the writers in this book do not always look at the same things. Yet, however various the movements and the kinds of people supporting them, the Progressive era rested on definable, widely shared, unifying principles. The first historian of that age of reform, Benjamin Parke De Witt, summed them up this way nearly fifty years ago:

> In this widespread political agitation that at first sight seems so inco-
> herent and chaotic, there may be distinguished upon examination and
> analysis three tendencies. The first of these tendencies is found in the
> insistence by the best men in all political parties that special, minority,
> and corrupt influence in government—national, state, and city—be re-
> moved; the second tendency is found in the demand that the structure or
> machinery of government, which has hitherto been admirably adapted to
> control by the few, be so changed and modified that it will be more
> difficult for the few, and easier for the many, to control; and, finally, the
> third tendency is found in the rapidly growing conviction that the func-
> tions of government at present are too restricted and that they must be
> increased and extended to relieve social and economic distress. These
> three tendencies with varying emphasis are seen to-day in the platform and
> program of every political party; they are manifested in the political
> changes and reforms that are advocated and made in the nation, the
> states, and the cities; and, because of their universality and definiteness,
> they may be said to constitute the real progressive movement.*

De Witt's book is still the fullest account of what his contemporaries were trying to do, but he was too close to his times to raise questions that have since interested scholars. Concerned only with "the movement," he did not ask what kinds of people went into it. Was there a Progressive personality? Nor could he, writing before the record was in, evaluate the results of Progressive changes

---

* *The Progressive Movement: A Non-Partisan, Comprehensive Discussion of Current Tendencies in American Politics* (New York, 1915), pp. 4–5.

in the economy, politics, social relations, and culture. What are the achievements and the failures of the Progressive era? And because he believed in
Progressive values as an unmixed good when so many other Americans did,
De Witt felt no need to be introspective about those values. Were they as
worthy as he assumed them to be?

Answers to the above questions have varied over the past forty-odd years
in direct ratio to the influences that govern historical interpretations in general: the writer's knowledge, his ability to handle evidence, his skill in asking
imaginative questions, his angle of vision, and his times. For each aspect of
the Progressive era examined in this book (foreign policy is left out for reasons
of space), there are at least two opposing points of view.

Vernon L. Parrington and John Chamberlain open the debate with interpretations of the Progressive era as a whole. Parrington, himself a Progressive,
celebrates his generation for reviving the humanitarian passion of the 1830s
and 1840s—America's first great age of reform—and for coping realistically with
the problems of the modern world. Chamberlain, a young Marxist of the
1930s, derides the Progressives for promoting reforms that reformed nothing.
We have here a classical Progressive defense and a classical leftist attack. To
Parrington the Progressive era was an obvious liberal renaissance, whereas to
Chamberlain it was an archetypal liberal failure.

The three historians following Parrington and Chamberlain deal with the
most baffling, the most frustrating, the most treacherous, but also the most
fascinating problem in historical analysis: the problem of causation. No one
has ever seen a cause; it is not a thing but an idea of how things are con-
nected. It is a human construct, a mental contrivance, an abstraction designed
to give order and meaning to experience. In history a cause can be an event
or an idea, a push or a pull, a force or a motive, a long tradition or a chance
happening. But no matter what the historian thinks it is, he must relate it
concretely to actual human beings. That is what John D. Hicks, George E.
Mowry, and J. Joseph Huthmacher try to do in their selections. Each of them,
however, singles out a different social group as being the most important
originator of the Progressive program: radical farmers, the urban elite, the
big-city masses.

The oldest interpretation, represented by Hicks and found in most textbooks down to this day, is that Progressivism issued from Populism. This was
a popular idea among reformers themselves during the first part of the
century. William Allen White, a Bull Mooser in 1912, put it this way: the
Progressives "caught the Populists in swimming and stole all their clothing
except the frayed underdrawers of free silver." Professor Hicks documented
the point so convincingly in *The Populist Revolt* (1931), revealing the striking
resemblance between Populist demands and Progressive legislation, that until
recently few historians doubted that the intellectual parents of the Progressives
were agrarian reformers.

The belief that Progressivism was essentially Populism with the hayseed removed (to paraphrase still another remark by William Allen White) has been challenged during the past fifteen years. Several historians, discovering that urban liberals in the 1880s and 1890s held reform views identical to the Populists', have concluded that the nineteenth-century origins of Progressivism lay in the cities as well as on the farms. Other writers have gone so far as to read Populism out of the liberal fraternity altogether, claiming that Populist provincialism, isolationism, racialism, and irrationalism sowed the seeds for subsequent right-wing groups. The interpretation denying links between Populism and Progressivism selected for this book, expounded by Professor Mowry, locates the Progressive impulse in the character of its leaders: the gentry of the cities.

More specifically, resenting labor leaders, political bosses, and robber barons for threatening their status, power, and values, the gentry generated movements for social justice, clean government, and regulated capitalism. This thesis, owing to a striking term coined by Richard Hofstadter, is now known as the "status-revolution" thesis. But it was no sooner accepted than J. Joseph Huthmacher, who is junior to Mowry by the same number of years that Mowry is to Hicks, entered the lists to challenge it. The reform thrust came not merely from the scions of old families on the defensive, he argues, but more significantly from the non-Anglo-Saxon immigrant masses on the move.

The attitudes of old-stock American Progressives toward the melting pot is discussed by John Higham and Oscar Handlin. Immigrants and their children constituted a majority in most of the larger and medium-sized cities during the Progressive era, and prejudice was building up against them and would eventuate in restrictive legislation by the 1920s. Progressives approached the newcomers with mixed feelings. On the one hand, they desired to improve the slums, the home of immigrant poverty, while on the other, they hoped to destroy the political machine, the recipient of the immigrant vote. Did the Progressives foster nativism or did they fight it and remain loyal to the traditional, century-and-a-half liberal American policy of the open door? Higham gives one answer to that question and Handlin still another.

The Progressives also faced in two ways when they considered the kind of economy they wanted and the role that government should play in it. Their differences were dramatized by Theodore Roosevelt's New Nationalism and Woodrow Wilson's New Freedom in the election of 1912. Roosevelt regarded bigness in business as both historically inevitable and economically beneficial. He was prepared to regulate monopoly and also to expand the welfare functions of the state to take care of the laboring poor. But to Wilson large corporations were inefficient and, what is equally important, a threat to social mobility. He, too, would use the power of the federal government, but solely to break up the trusts and return to an older, more competitive, more individualistic economy of small enterprise.

Most historians who have written about the Progressive era favor the New Nationalism over the New Freedom. In this they echo such advanced intellectuals of the 1910s as Walter Lippmann and Herbert Croly of the *New Republic,* who argued that the need of the twentieth century is for organization, control, order, planning, and not a return to Manchester liberalism. Yet liberal scholars have managed to acclaim Wilson as well as Roosevelt. The current consensus, herein expressed by the New Deal historian, Arthur M. Schlesinger, Jr., is that President Wilson implemented the New Nationalism once in office.

Richard Hofstadter, who is to the left of both Progressivism and the New Deal, should be read as a rebuttal to Schlesinger. He contends that the Wilson administration fulfilled its own New Freedom promises and, what is more, that Roosevelt was no less nostalgic than Wilson for an unreturnable past. But of all the writers who have attacked Roosevelt as a pseudo liberal, none has done so more violently than H. L. Mencken, a humanist but not a humanitarian. His remarks on TR's love of order and discipline deserve a particularly careful reading, for the problem of liberty and authority in a free society is by no means resolved today. The final piece in this section, by John Braeman, is a useful summary of current historical opinion about the Progressive legacy regarding government and the economy.

The last two readings are about why the Progressive movement ended and what happened to it during the 1920s. According to Parrington and his disciples, World War I blighted the hopes of a humanitarian generation and prepared the ground for the age of normalcy. This interpretation, William E. Leuchtenburg contends, makes too much of external causes and not enough of the internal weaknesses within Progressivism itself. His view of the Progressive movement in the 1920s as "tired" is, in turn, challenged by Arthur S. Link, who cites evidence pointing toward a continuing vitality. Leuchtenburg and Link restate, but in a different form, the controversy with which this book begins.

The problem examined in these pages is of more than historiographical interest. Today every underdeveloped nation—which is to say the majority of the world's population—wants to create a technological civilization. It is unlikely that they will do so without confronting social problems similar to those that Americans faced during their take-off point. The Progressives and their contemporaries had to make hard choices between this or that immigration policy, economic policy, government policy. How well did they choose? The student of history can not avoid that question, for he has the obligation not only of recreating the past as it probably was but of placing a judgment on it. He, too, must choose in deciding whether the Progressive era was a liberal renaissance or a liberal failure. And that involves, in addition to knowledge and understanding, moral values.

VERNON L. PARRINGTON (1871–1929), the Kansas-bred son of a Union Army captain, was the outstanding intellectual historian of his generation. Like Charles Beard and Frederick Jackson Turner, fellow Midwestern scholars to whom he was intellectually indebted, he interpreted the American past as a recurrent struggle to achieve the open society against special privilege. In the fragment below from his unfinished lifetime's work, of which the first two volumes won a Pulitzer Prize in 1928, the Progressive partisan justifies his generation's fight against plutocracy. Note how he links Progressivism to a previous reform era.*

The Progressive Era: A Liberal Renaissance

The great movement of liberalism that took possession of the American mind after the turn of the century—a movement not unworthy to be compared with the ferment of the eighteen forties—was the spontaneous reaction of an America still only half urbanized, still clinging to ideals and ways of an older simpler America, to an industrialism that was driving its plowshare through the length and breadth of the familiar scene, turning under the rude furrows what before had been growing familiarly there. It was the first reaction of America to the revolutionary change that followed upon the exhaustion of the frontier—an attempt to secure through the political state the freedoms that before had come from unpreempted opportunity.

For a quarter of a century following the great westward expansion of the late sixties America had been drifting heedlessly towards a different social order. The shambling frontier democracy that had sufficed an earlier time was visibly breaking down in presence of the imperious power of a centralizing capitalism. The railways were a dramatic embodiment of the new machine civilization that was running head on into a primitive social organism fashioned by the old domestic economy, and the disruptions and confusions were a warning that the country was in for vast changes. New masters, new ways. The rule of the captain of industry had come. The farmers had long been in ugly mood, but their great rebellion was put down in 1896, and never again could they hope to wrest sovereignty from capitalism. The formal adoption of the gold standard in 1900 served notice to the world that America had put away its democratic agrarianism, that a shambling Jacksonian individualism had had its day, and that henceforth the destiny of the country lay in the hands of its business men. Capitalism was master of the country and though for the present it was content to use the political machinery of democracy it was driving towards an objective that was the negation of democracy.

The immediate reaction to so broad a shift in the course of manifest destiny was a growing uneasiness amongst the middle class—small business and professional men—who looked with fear upon the program of the captains of industry. Industrialization brought its jars and upsets. The little fish did not enjoy being swallowed by the big, and as they watched the movement of economic centralization encroaching on the field of competition they saw the doors of opportunity closing to them. It was to this great body of *petite bourgeoisie* that members of the lesser intellectuals—journalists, sociologists, reformers—were to make appeal. The work was begun dramatically with the spectacularly advertised *Frenzied Finance,* written by Thomas W. Lawson, and appearing as a series in *McClure's Magazine* in 1903. The immense popular success of the venture proved that the fire was ready for the fat, and at once a host of volunteer writers fell to feeding the flames. The new ten-cent magazines provided the necessary vehicle of publicity, and enterprising editors were soon increasing their circulations with every issue. As it became evident how popular was the chord that had been struck, more competent workmen joined themselves to the group of journalists: novelists—a growing army of them—essayists, historians, political scientists, philosophers, a host of heavy-armed troops that moved forward in a frontal attack on the strongholds of the new plutocracy. Few writers in the years between 1903 and 1917 escaped being drawn into the movement—an incorrigible romantic perhaps, like the young James Branch Cabell, or a cool patrician like Edith Wharton; and with such popular novelists as Winston Churchill, Robert Herrick, Ernest Poole, David Graham Phillips, Upton Sinclair, and Jack London embellishing the rising liberalism with dramatic heroes and villains, and dressing their salads with the wickedness of Big Business; with such political leaders as Bob La Follette and Theodore Roosevelt and Woodrow Wilson beating up the remotest villages for recruits; with such scholars as Thorstein Veblen, Charles A. Beard, and John Dewey, and such lawyers as Louis Brandeis, Frank P. Walsh, and Samuel Untermyer, the movement gathered such momentum and quickened such a ferment as had not been known before in the lands since the days of the Abolition controversy. The mind and conscience of America were stirred to their lowest sluggish stratum, and a democratic renaissance was all aglow on the eastern horizon.

At the core it was a critical realistic movement that spread quietly amongst intellectuals, but the nebulous tail of the comet blazed across the sky for all to wonder at: and it was the tail rather than the core that aroused the greatest immediate interest. Lincoln Steffens, Charles Edward Russell, Ida Tarbell, Gustavus Myers, and Upton Sinclair were read eagerly because they dealt with themes that many were interested in—the political machine, watered stock, Standard Oil, the making of great fortunes, and the like—and they invested their exposures with the dramatic interest of a detective story. Up to 1910 it was largely a muckraking movement—to borrow President Roosevelt's picturesque phrase; a time of brisk housecleaning that searched out old cobwebs and disturbed the dust that lay thick on the antiquated furniture. The Gilded Age had been slovenly and such a housecleaning was long overdue. There was a vast amount of nosing about to discover bad smells, and to sensitive noses the bad smells seemed to be everywhere. Evidently some hidden cesspool was fouling American life, and as the inquisitive plumbers tested the household drains they came upon the source of infection—not one cesspool but many, under every city hall and beneath every state capitol—dug secretly by politicians in the pay of respectable business men. It was these cesspools that were poisoning the national household, and there would be no health in America till they were filled in and no others dug.

It was a dramatic discovery and when the corruption of American politics was laid on the threshold of business—like a bastard on the doorsteps of the father— a tremendous disurbance resulted. There was a great fluttering and clamor amongst the bats and owls, an ominous creaking of the machine as the wrenches were thrown into the well-oiled wheels, and a fierce sullen anger at the hue and cry set up. To many honest Americans the years between 1903 and 1910 were abusive and scurrilous beyond decency, years when no man and no business, however honorable, was safe from the pillory; when wholesale exposure had grown profitable to sensation-mongers, and great reputations were lynched by vigilantes and reputable corporations laid under indictment at the bar of public opinion. Respectable citizens did not like to have their goodly city held up to the world as "corrupt and contented"; they did not like to have their municipal housekeeping brought into public disrepute no matter how sluttish it might be. It was not pleasant for members of great families to read a cynical history of the origins of their fortunes, or for railway presidents seeking political favors to find on the newsstand a realistic account of the bad scandals that had smirched their roads. It was worse than unpleasant, it was hurtful to business. And so quietly, and as speedily as could be done decently, the movement was brought to a stop by pressure put on the magazines that lent themselves to such harmful disclosures. Then followed a campaign of education. Responding to judicious instruction, conducted in the columns of the most respectable newspapers, the American public was soon brought to understand that it was not the muck that was harmful, but the indiscretion of those who commented in print on the bad smells. It was reckoned a notable triumph for sober and patriotic good sense.

So after a few years of amazing activity the muckraking movement came to a stop. But not before it had done its work; not before the American middle class had been indoctrinated in the elementary principles of political realism and had rediscovered the social conscience lost since the days of the Civil War. Many a totem had been thrown down by the irreverent hands of the muckrakers, and many a fetish held up to ridicule, and plutocracy in America would not recover its peace of mind until at great cost the totems should be set up again and the fetishes reanointed with the oil of sanctity. The substantial result of the movement was the instruction it afforded in the close kinship between business and politics—a lesson greatly needed by a people long fed on romantic unrealities. It did not crystallize for the popular mind in the broad principle of economic determinism; that remained for certain of the intellectuals to apply to American experience. But with its sordid object—service—it punished the flabby optimism of the Gilded Age, with its object-lessons in business politics; it revealed the hidden hand that was pulling the strings of the political puppets; it tarnished the gilding that had been carefully laid on our callous exploitation, and it brought under common suspicion the captain of industry who had risen as a national hero from the muck of individualism. It was a sharp guerilla attack on the sacred American System, but behind the thin skirmish-line lay a volunteer army that was making ready to deploy for a general engagement with plutocracy.

With the flood of light thrown upon the fundamental law by the historians, the movement of liberalism passed quickly through successive phases of thought. After the first startled surprise it set about the necessary business of acquainting the American people with its findings in the confident belief that a democratic electorate would speedily democratize the instrument. Of this first stage the late Professor J. Allen Smith's *The Spirit of American Government* (1907) was the most adequate expression, a work that greatly influenced the program of the rising Progressive Party. But changes came swiftly and within half a dozen years the movement had passed from political programs to economic, concerned not so greatly with political democracy as with economic democracy. Of this second phase Professor Beard's notable study, *An Economic Interpretation of the Constitution* (1913), was the greatest intellectual achievement. Underlying this significant work was a philosophy of politics that set it sharply apart from preceding studies—a philosophy that unsympathetic readers were quick to attribute to Karl Marx, but that in reality derived from sources far earlier and for Americans at least far more respectable. The current conception of the political state as determined in its form and activities by economic groups is no modern Marxian perversion of political theory; it goes back to Aristotle, it underlay the thinking of Harrington and Locke and the seventeenth-century English school, it shaped the conclusions of Madison and Hamilton and John Adams, it ran through all the discussions of the Constitutional Convention, and it reappeared in the arguments of Webster and Calhoun. It was the main-traveled road of political thought until a new highway was laid out by French engineers, who, disliking the bog of economics, surveyed another route by way of romantic equalitarianism. The logic of the engineers was excellent, but the drift of politics is little influenced by logic, and abstract equalitarianism proved to be poor material for highway construction. In divorcing political theory from contact with sobering reality it gave it over to a treacherous romanticism. In seeking to avoid the bog of economics it ran into an arid desert.

To get back once more on the main-traveled road, to put away all profitless romanticisms and turn realist, taking up again the method of economic interpretation unused in America since the days of Webster and Calhoun, became therefore the business of the second phase of liberalism to which Professor Beard applied himself. The earlier group of liberals were ill equipped to wage successful war against plutocracy. Immersed in the traditional equalitarian philosophy, they underestimated the strength of the enemies of democracy. They did not realize what legions of Swiss Guards property can summon to its defense. They were still romantic idealists tilting at windmills, and it was to bring them to a sobering sense of reality that *The Economic Interpretation of the Constitution* was written. If property is the master force in every society one cannot understand American institutional development until one has come to understand the part property played in shaping the fundamental law. Interpreted thus the myths that had gathered about the Constitution fell away of themselves and the document was revealed as English rather than French, the judicious expression of substantial eighteenth-century realism that accepted the property basis of political action, was skeptical of romantic idealisms, and was more careful to protect title-deeds to legal holdings than to claim unsurveyed principalities in Utopia. If therefore liberalism were to accomplish any substantial results it must approach its problems in the same realistic spirit, recognizing the masterful ambitions of property, recruiting democratic forces to overmaster the Swiss

Guards, leveling the strongholds that property had erected within the organic law, and taking care that no new strongholds should rise. The problem confronting liberalism was the problem of the subjection of property to social justice.

Yet interesting as was the muckraking tail of the comet, far more significant was the core—the substantial body of knowledge gathered by the scholars and flung into the scale of public opinion. The realities of the American past had been covered deep with layers of patriotic myths, provided in simpler days when the young Republic, suffering from a natural inferiority complex, was building up a defense against the acrid criticism of Tory Europe. Those myths had long since served their purpose and had become a convenient refuge for the bats and owls of the night; it was time to strip them away and apply to the past objective standards of scholarship, and to interpret it in the light of an adequate philosophy of history. To this work, so essential to any intelligent understanding of the American experiment, a group of historians and political scientists turned with competent skill, and the solid results of their labor remained after the popular ferment subsided, as a foundation for later liberals to build on.

The journalistic muckrakers had demonstrated that America was not in fact the equalitarian democracy it professed to be, and the scholars supplemented their work by tracing to its historical source the weakness of the democratic principle in governmental practice. America had never been a democracy for the sufficient reason that too many handicaps had been imposed upon the majority will. The democratic principle had been bound with withes like Samson and had become a plaything for the Philistines. From the beginning—the scholars discovered—democracy and property had been at bitter odds; the struggle invaded the Constitutional Convention, it gave form to the party alignment between Hamilton and Jefferson, Jackson and Clay, and then during the slavery struggle, sinking underground like a lost river, it nevertheless had determined party conflicts down to the present. In this ceaseless conflict between the man and the dollar, between democracy and property, the reasons for persistent triumph of property were sought in the provisions of the organic law, and from a critical study of the Constitution came a discovery that struck home like a submarine torpedo—the discovery that the drift toward plutocracy was not a drift away from the spirit of the Constitution, but an inevitable unfolding from its premises; that instead of having been conceived by the fathers as a democratic instrument, it had been conceived in a spirit designedly hostile to democracy; that it was, in fact, a carefully formulated expression of eighteenth-century property consciousness, erected as a defense against the democratic spirit that had got out of hand during the Revolution, and that the much-praised system of checks and balances was designed and intended for no other end than a check on the political power of the majority—a power acutely feared by the property consciousness of the times.

It was a startling discovery that profoundly stirred the liberal mind of the early years of the century; yet the really surprising thing is that it should have come as a surprise. It is not easy to understand today why since Civil War days intelligent Americans should so strangely have confused the Declaration of Independence and the Constitution, and have come to accept them as complementary statements of the democratic purpose of America. Their unlikeness is unmistakable: the one a classical statement of French humanitarian democracy, the other an organic law designed to safeguard the minority under republican rule. The confusion must be charged in part to the lawyers who had taken over the custodianship of the Constitution, and in part to the florid romantic temper of the middle nineteenth century. When the fierce slavery struggle fell into the past, whatever honest realism had risen from the passions of the times was buried with the dead issue. The militant attacks on the Constitution so common in Abolitionist circles after 1835, and the criticism of the Declaration that was a part of the southern argument, were both forgotten, and with the Union reestablished by force of arms, the idealistic cult of the fundamental law entered on a second youth. In the blowsy Gilded Age the old myths walked the land again, wrapped in battle-torn flags and appealing to the blood shed on southern battlefields. It was not till the advent of a generation unblinded by the passions of civil war that the Constitution again was examined critically, and the earlier charge of the Abolitionists that it was designed to serve property rather than men, was heard once more. But this time with far greater weight of evidence behind it. As the historians dug amongst the contemporary records they came upon a mass of fact the Abolitionists had been unaware of. The evidence was written so plainly, in such explicit and incontrovertible words—not only in *Elliott's Debates,* but in the minutes of the several State Conventions, in contemporary letters and memoirs, in newspapers and pamphlets and polite literature—that it seemed incredible that honest men could have erred so greatly in confusing the Constitution with the Declaration.

...In its reaction to industrialism America had reached the point Chartist England had reached in the eighteen-forties and Marxian Germany in the eighteen-seventies. That was before a mechanistic science had laid its heavy discouragements on the drafters of democratic programs. Accepting the principle of economic determinism, liberalism still clung to its older democratic teleology, convinced that somehow economic determinism would turn out to be a fairy godmother to the proletariat and that from the imperious drift of industrial expansion must eventually issue social justice. Armed with this faith liberalism threw itself into the work of cleaning the Augean stables, and its reward came in the achievements of President Wilson's first administration.

Then the war intervened and the green fields shriveled in an afternoon. With the cynicism that came with postwar days the democratic liberalism of 1917 was thrown away like an empty whiskey-flask. Clever young men began to make merry over democracy. It was preposterous, they said, to concern oneself about social justice; nobody wants social justice. The first want of every man, as John Adams remarked a hundred years ago, is his dinner, and the second his girl. Out of the muck of the war had come a great discovery—so it was reported—the discovery that psychology as well as economics has its word to say on politics. From the army intelligence tests the moron emerged as a singular commentary on our American democracy, and with the discovery of the moron the democratic principle was

in for a slashing attack. Almost overnight an army of enemies was marshaled against it. The eugenist with his isolated germ theory flouted the perfectional psychology of John Locke, with its emphasis on environment as the determining factor in social evolution—a psychology on which the whole idealistic interpretation was founded; the beardless philosopher discovered Nietzsche and in his pages found the fit master of the moron—the biological aristocrat who is the flower that every civilization struggles to produce; the satirist discovered the flatulent reality that is middle-class America and was eager to thrust his jibes at the complacent denizens of the Valley of Democracy. Only the behaviorist, with his insistence on the plasticity of the new-born child, offers some shreds of comfort to the democrat; but he quickly takes them away again with his simplification of conduct to imperious drives that stamp men as primitive animals. If the mass— the raw materials of democracy—never rises much above sex appeals and belly needs, surely it is poor stuff to try to work up into an excellent civilization, and the dreams of the social idealist who forecasts a glorious democratic future are about as substantial as moonshine. It is a discouraging essay. Yet it is perhaps conceivable that our current philosophy —the brilliant coruscations of our younger intelligentsia—may indeed not prove to be the last word in social philosophy. Perhaps—is this lèse-majesté—when our youngest liberals have themselves come to the armchair age they will be smiled at in turn by sons who are still cleverer and who will find their wisdom as foolish as the wisdom of 1917 seems to them today. But that lies on the knees of the gods.

The reaction of young intellectuals against the Progressive era that troubled Parrington in the 1920s culminated early in the 1930s with the publication of *Farewell to Reform* by JOHN CHAMBERLAIN (1903–). A journalist since his graduation from Yale College in 1925, the New Haven-born writer has been a constant critic of American liberalism. Today he contributes to the right-wing *National Review,* whereas in the 1930s he was a Marxist publicist. In the selection that follows, Chamberlain's rejection of Progressivism as naïve and ineffective should be read as a socialist call to action against both liberalism and fascism during the Great Depression.*

► ‖ *On the Art of Liberal Failure*

And so we come to the end of the Progressive trail. What have the years left with us? Their reverberations have bequeathed to us what might be called, with proper obeisance to Lewis Mumford, a Little Golden Day of general culture, with satire at its base. This culture has been the more adventurous because of the spirit of general dissent and inquiry that begot it. But since this book is concerned only with that culture which, on the plane of ideas, has served as carrier of the notions shaping the direct development of the politics of the Progressive epoch, the end-product of the Little Golden Day need not concern us here.

The results, or lack of results, of the Progressive years in government and interrelated business are, however, our direct concern. There are some—such as the good William Allen White, and Charles Edward Russell—who consider that American industry has been suffused with Progressive shibboleths; we have been saved, they aver, from a harsh industrial tyranny by the stirrings of the Rooseveltian and Wilsonian years. This is not an opinion to be dismissed with a sneer. Al Smith's factory legislation, the pure food laws, workmen's compensation, and so on, have done some humanizing. The Morgan trick of taking in the public as investors, the idea of which had a grand burgeoning after the success of the government in floating the Liberty Loan bond issues, is beneficent in one sense, although in a larger sense it is unfortunate, since it paralyzes the will to radical action when radical action is needed. There have been honest efforts directed toward instituting a humane science of industrial management, notably in the Procter and Gamble Company, the Hart, Schaffner and Marx Company, the Baltimore and Ohio railroad equipment shops, the manufacturing company of Henry Dennison of Framingham, Mass. Mr. E. A. Filene, given his way, could, no doubt, do much to integrate the spirit of humane rationalism with the spirit of business.

But the ghost of the Veblen who knew, better than Lippmann, the import of the phrase, "well-meaning but unmeaning," will not down; the very nature of business, which is, fundamentally, based on the desire for profits, works to undermine the advance guard of the Filenes and the Dennisons. Faced with a loss, only the most Quixotic man of business can indulge in positive humanitarian tactics. Consciences may be salved by the practice of hiring outside efficiency experts to do firing and wage cutting, but the results are the same. Work may be "shared" and staggered, but sharing on the basis of stationary or diminished total wages per week does not increase purchasing power. The Progressive business man, individually humane, is caught in a complicated net of aggregate weave. He cannot cut clear by himself. In business, in time of trouble, the most unscrupulous inevitably set the pace for the whole

machine, just as in good times the ones out for the immediate gain set the pace.

As for Progressive government, the results of the three decades of strife antecedent to 1919 are, perhaps, minimal. Oswald Garrison Villard thinks we are no further along the road than we were in 1900. This, I think, is susceptible of proof—and, to boot, we are on the wrong road. If you think the tariff is at the bottom of our troubles, it is to be noted that the tariff is still sky-high. But even if we had a low tariff, it is doubtful that it could have stemmed the down-thrust of depression. The Underwood tariff of 1913 did not prevent us from limping industrially until the War created a market for American goods. Free trade, in the long run, cannot prevent a dynamic capitalistic industrial machine from glutting markets as the upcurve of greed succeeds the downcurve of fear in the psychological cycle that is the concomitant of the business cycle.

The pet political solutions of the Progressives, designed to make government more responsible to the will of the electorate, have notoriously been weak reeds. The initiative and the referendum have produced nothing. Woman suffrage has only added, in direct proportion, to Republican and Democratic totals. Direct primaries have proved not even a palliative; they have worked against strong labor and independent party organization, which is the only hope of labor and the consumer in the political field. As Paul Douglas says, where parties are closed organizations, as in England, nominations are made by local nuclei of party workers who know what they want. If a group dislikes the candidates of existing party machines, the only recourse is to put a candidate of its own in the field. The direct primary seemingly weakens the necessity for this; it creates the illusion that in inert "people," spasmodically led, can be aroused to holding the machine politician in line by the threat that they may turn on him at the primary polls. The result is . . . the machine politician promises much, does little . . . and the people are let down. During a two, or four, or six, year period of office-holding, there is much time for an electorate to forget.

The popular election of Senators, instituted in 1913, has made very little actual difference. The real difference between the type of Senator that flourished in the days of the McKinley plutocracy and the type of the present is one of demagoguery; the modern Senator, representing the same interests as his legislature-elected predecessor, is compelled to be a master of the art of obfuscation. Senator Nelson Aldrich, in the 1890 dispensation, could afford to leave the obfuscation to his local manipulator, General Brayton, who kept the legislature in line while his master attended to more important business.

The real human gain of Woodrow Wilson's Administration was the domestication of the eight-hour day in many areas of industry, made possible by the Adamson Law rendering it compulsory on the railroads. The Federal Reserve system is, beyond doubt, better than the previous banking system. It is flexible, it is an instrument which, through its control of the rediscount rate, can take up the slack between productive activity, and speculation at any time *if it is properly run*. But, in setting down these gains, we have about exhausted the really important positive legislation of thirty years. The business cycle remains; until that is done away with, all legislation looking to the welfare of the common man must appear in the light of small, temporary oscillations along the course of a major graph.

This brings us to the definition of "reform," and its alternative, revolution. Now, revolution (change of structure and aims) inevitably carries with it connotations of untoward happenings, of barricades or whatever may be their twentieth-century equivalent, of whatever modern ingenuity can devise as substitute for the guillotine, of the reign of terror induced by the menace of counter-revolution. To Stuart Chase, it means a sudden sharp disruption of the distributive mechanism of an entire nation.

Personally, I experience none of the psychological thrill which hopes of "the revolution" send tingling through the born radical. I am as timorous in the face of physical violence as Mr. Bernard Shaw. Because of this fact, it may be that I am indulging in wishful thinking when I say that I am not persuaded that votes will not do. It seems to me that, in a nation of forty-eight organized State governments, with forty-eight militias, votes *must* do. I am mindful of the good old revolutionary axiom that no owning class ever gave up its property and preferred position without a struggle. Yet there are revolutions *and* revolutions; and there are ways *and* ways of confiscation, even in the face of the Fifth and Fourteenth Amendments. There is the revolution advocated (but not worked out in its implications) by Mr. Kenneth Burke—the revolution by indirection. An income of six per cent may be shaved to the vanishing point by a five per cent system of taxation, as will be necessary if the toll of technological unemployment in agriculture and industry grows. Such a system of taxation would sorely cripple the re-investment process—which, in turn, would help bring closer the day of total legal confiscation of productive private property (with the exception of small farm holdings). In the light of the possibilities which the Seventeenth (Income Tax) Amendment, one of the negative triumphs of the Progressive epoch, has opened up for bloodless revolution in this country, I affirm the hope, in bidding farewell to reform, that parliamentary processes will not fail in the interim leading up to the necessary class shifts in control.

But, one fancies the reader asking, are not parliamentary methods the very essence of reform? This depends upon the definition of the word. In the United States, "reform"—apart from the meaning pumped into it by the Anti-Saloon Leaguers and other specifically "moral" reformers, who are beyond the scope of this inquiry—has always had a "return" connotation. By "reform," a host of political leaders, Bryan, La Follette, Wilson, Theodore Roosevelt at times, and Franklin D. Roosevelt to-day, have hoped to "return" to the ways of their fathers— to the methods and possibilities of a more primitive capitalism. As Walter Lippmann remarked of the Wilson of *The New Freedom,* they have seen the laborer as a possible shopkeeper. That is why Progressivism and Liberalism in this country are, at the moment, preparing the ground for an American Fascism;

they have been identified with the shop-keeper instincts of the common citizen, who is willing to make his trade with the "big fellow" if he can retain a privilege or two.

The curbing of the "money power," the abolition of "privilege," the opening up of opportunity by the Single Tax, the redemption of the promises of the New Freedom, all of these have been made the basis for a "return" demand— a demand for the evocation and reëstablishment of a vanished, and somehow more "moral" and "honest" *status quo.* And all economic reforms that have been undertaken in the spirit of Bryan, of La Follette, of Wilson, have worked in a way precisely against the grain of Progressive or neo-democratic hopes; instead of "freeing" the common man within the capitalistic system, these reforms have made the system, as a long-run proposition, more difficult of operation; and this, in turn, has reacted upon the common man as employee, as small bond-holder, as savings-account depositor, as insurance-policy owner. The value of reforms, as I see it, is that they fail to achieve what they are sanguinely intended to achieve; and in so failing they help make the system which they are intended to patch up only the more unpatchable. In other words, every vote for reform, entered upon intelligently, is a Jesuitical vote for revolution.

JOHN D. HICKS (1890–   ), professor emeritus at the
University of California in Berkeley, is best known
among scholars for his work on farmers' movements in
his native Midwest. Born in Missouri and educated at
Northwestern and the University of Wisconsin, he
wrote the *Populist Revolt* while teaching at the
University of Nebraska. That book was influenced,
Professor Hicks has since pointed out, by "my
observation of the raw deal that the farmers were
getting in the 1920s." The article reproduced here,
substantially the same as the concluding chapter in
Hicks' monograph, is the classical argument for linking
Populism to Progressivism as cause and effect.*

Populist Origins

Early in 1890, when the People's party was yet in the embryo stage, a farmer editor from the West set forth the doctrine that "The Cranks Always Win." As he saw it,

The cranks are those who do not accept the existing order of things, and propose to change them. The existing order of things is always accepted by the majority, therefore the cranks are always in the minority. They are always progressive thinkers and always in advance of their time, and they always win. Called fanatics and fools at first, they are sometimes persecuted and abused. But their reforms are generally righteous, and time, reason and argument bring men to their side.

Abused and ridiculed, then tolerated, then respectfully given a hearing, then supported. This has been the gauntlet that all great reforms and reformers have run, from Gallileo to John Brown.

The writer of this editorial may have overstated his case, but a backward glance at the history of Populism shows that many of the reforms that the Populists demanded, while despised and rejected for a season, won out triumphantly in the end. The party itself did not survive, nor did many of its leaders, although the number of contemporary politicians whose escutcheons should bear

* John D. Hicks, "The Persistence of Populism," *Minnesota History*, XII (March 1931),
3–20. Reprinted by permission of the Minnesota Historical Society.

the bend sinister of Populism is larger than might be supposed; but Populistic doctrines showed an amazing vitality.

In formulating their principles the Populists reasoned that the ordinary, honest, willing American worker, be he farmer or be he laborer, might expect in this land of opportunity not only the chance to work, but also as the rightful reward of his labor a fair degree of prosperity. When, in the later eighties and in the "heart-breaking nineties," hundreds of thousands—perhaps millions—of men found themselves either without work to do, or having work, unable to pay their just debts and make a living, the Populists held that there must be "wrong and crime and fraud somewhere." What was more natural than to fix the blame for this situation upon the manufacturers, the railroads, the money-lenders, the middlemen—plutocrats all, whose "colossal fortunes, unprecedented in the history of mankind" grew ever greater while the multitudes came to know the meaning of want? Work was denied when work might well be given, and "the fruits of the toil of millions were boldly stolen."

And the remedy? In an earlier age the hard-pressed farmers and laborers might have fled to free farms in the seemingly limitless lands of the West, but now the era of free lands had passed. Where, then, might they look for help? Where, if not to the government, which alone had the power to bring the mighty oppressors of the people to bay? So to the government the Populists turned. From it they asked laws to insure a full redress of grievances. As Professor Frederick J. Turner puts it, "the defenses of the pioneer democrat began to shift from free land to legislation, from the ideal of individualism to the ideal of social con-

trol through regulation by law." Unfortunately, however, the agencies of government had been permitted to fall into the hands of the plutocrats. Hence, if the necessary corrective legislation were to be obtained, the people must first win control of their government. The Populist philosophy thus boiled down finally to two fundamental propositions: one, that the government must restrain the selfish tendencies of those who profited at the expense of the poor and needy; the other, that the people, not the plutocrats, must control the government.

In their efforts to remove all restrictions on the power of the people to rule the Populists accepted as their own a wide range of reforms. They believed, and on this they had frequently enough the evidence of their own eyes, that corruption existed at the ballot box and that a fair count was often denied. They fell in, therefore, with great enthusiasm when agitators, who were not necessarily Populists, sought to popularize the Australian ballot and such other measures as were calculated to insure a true expression of the will of the people. Believing as they did that the voice of the people was the voice of God, they sought to eliminate indirect elections, especially the election of United States senators by state legislatures and the president and the vice president by an electoral college. Fully aware of the habits of party bosses in manipulating nominating conventions, the Populists veered more and more toward direct primary elections, urging in some of their later platforms that nominations even for president and vice president should be made by direct vote. Woman suffrage was a delicate question, for it was closely identified with the politically hazardous matter of temperance legislation, but, after all, the idea of votes for women was so clearly in line with the Populist doctrine of popular rule that it could not logically be denied a place among genuinely Populistic reforms. Direct legislation through the initiative and referendum and through the easy amendment of state constitutions naturally appealed strongly to the Populists—the more so as they saw legislatures fail repeatedly to enact reform laws to which a majority of their members had been definitely pledged. "A majority of the people," declared the Sioux Falls convention, "can never be corruptly influenced." The recall of faithless officials, even judges, also attracted favorable attention from the makers of later Populist platforms.

To list these demands is to cite the chief political departures made in the United States during recent times. The Australian system of voting, improved registration laws, and other devices for insuring "a free ballot and a fair count" have long since swept the country. Woman suffrage has won an unqualifed victory. The election of United States senators by direct vote of the people received the approval of far more than two-thirds of the national House of Representatives as early as 1898; it was further foreshadowed by the adoption in a number of states, beginning in 1904, of senatorial primaries the results of which were to be regarded as morally binding upon the legislatures concerned; and it became a fact in 1913 with the ratification of the seventeenth amendment to the Constitution. The direct election of president and vice president was hard to reconcile with state control of the election machinery and state definition of the right to vote, hence this reform never caught on; but the danger of one presidential candidate receiving a majority of the popular vote and another a majority of the electoral vote, as was the case in the Cleveland-Harrison contest of 1888, seems definitely to have passed. Late elections may not prove that the popular voice always speaks intelligently; but they do seem to show that it speaks decisively. In the widespread use of the primary election for the making of party nominations, the Populist principle of popular rule has scored perhaps its most telling victory. Benjamin R. Tillman urged this reform in South Carolina at a very early date, but on obtaining control of the Democratic political machine of his state, he hesitated to give up the power which the convention system placed in his hands. At length, however, in 1896 he allowed the reform to go through. Wisconsin, spurred on by the La Follette forces, adopted the direct primary plan of nominations in 1903, and thereafter the other states of the Union, with remarkably few exceptions, fell into line. Presidential preference primaries, through which it was hoped that the direct voice of the people could be heard in the making of nominations for president and vice president, were also adopted by a number of states, beginning with Oregon in 1910. Direct legislation by the people became almost an obsession with the Populists, especially the middle-of-the-road faction, in whose platforms it tended to overshadow nearly every other issue; and it is perhaps significant that the initiative and referendum were adopted by South Dakota, a state in which the Populist party had shown great strength, as close on the heels of the Populist movement as 1898. Other states soon followed the South Dakota lead, and particularly in Oregon the experiment of popular legislation was given a thorough trial. New constitutions and numerous amendments to old constitutions tended also to introduce much popularly made law, the idea that legislation in a constitution is improper and unwise receiving perhaps its most shattering blow when an Oklahoma convention wrote for that state a constitution of fifty thousand words. The recall of elected officials has been applied chiefly in municipal affairs, but some states also permit its use for state officers and a few allow even judges, traditionally held to be immune from popular reactions, to be subjected to recall. Thus many of the favorite ideas of the Populists, ideas which had once been "abused and ridiculed," were presently "respectfully given a hearing, then supported."

Quite apart from these changes in the American form of government, the populist propaganda in favor of independent voting did much to undermine the intense party loyalties that had followed in the wake of the Civil War. The time had been when for the Republican voter "To doubt Grant was as bad as to doubt Christ," when the man who scratched his party ticket was regarded as little if any better than the traitor to his country. The Farmers' Alliance in its day had sought earnestly to wean the partisan voter over to independence. It had urged its members to "favor and assist to office such candidates only as are thoroughly identified with our principles and who will insist on such legislation as shall make them effective." And in this regard the Alliance, as some of its leaders boasted, had been a "great educator of the people." The Populist party had to go even further, for its growth depended almost wholly upon its ability to bring voters to a complete renunciation of old party loyalties. Since at one time or another well over a million men cast their ballots for Populist tickets, the loosening

of party ties that thus set in was of formidable proportions. Indeed, the man who became a Populist learned his lesson almost too well. When confronted, as many Populist voters thought themselves to be in 1896, with a choice between loyalty to party and loyalty to principle, the third-party adherent generally tended to stand on principle. Thereafter, as Populism faded out, the men who once had sworn undying devotion to the Omaha platform were compelled again to transfer their allegiance. Many Republicans became Democrats via the Populist route; many Democrats became Republicans. Probably, however, most of the Populists returned to the parties from which they had withdrawn, but party ties, once broken, were not so strong as they had been before. The rapid passing of voters from one party to another and the wholesale scratching of ballots, so characteristic of voting today, are distinctly reminiscent of Populism; as are also the frequent nonpartisan ballots by which judges, city commissioners, and other officers are now chosen wholly without regard to their party affiliations.

In the South the Populist demands for popular government produced a peculiar situation. To a very great extent the southern Populists were recruited from the rural classes, which had hitherto been politically inarticulate. Through the Populist party the "wool hat boys" from the country sought to obtain the weight in southern politics that their numbers warranted but that the "Bourbon" dynasties had ever denied them. In the struggle that ensued both sides made every possible use of the Negro vote, and the bugaboo of Negro domination was once again raised. Indeed, the experience of North Carolina under a combination government of Populists and Republicans furnished concrete evidence of what might happen should the political power of the Negro be restored. Under the circumstances, therefore, there seemed to be nothing for the white Populists to do but to return to their former allegiance until the menace of the Negro voter could be removed. With the Democratic party again supreme, the problem of Negro voting was attacked with right good will. Indeed, as early as 1890 the state of Mississippi, stimulated no doubt by the agitation over the Force Bill, adopted a constitution which fixed as a prerequisite for voting two years' residence in the state and one year's residence in the district or town. This provision, together with a poll tax that had to be paid far in advance of the dates set for elections, diminished appreciably the number of Negro voters, among whom indigence was common and the migratory propensity well developed. To complete the work of disfranchisement an amendment was added to the Mississippi constitution in 1892 which called for a modified literacy test that could be administered in such a way as to permit illiterate whites to vote, while discriminating against illiterate, or even literate blacks. The Tillmanites in South Carolina found legal means to exclude the Negro voter in 1895; Louisiana introduced her famous "grandfather clause" in 1898; North Carolina adopted residence, poll tax, and educational qualifications in 1900; Alabama followed in 1901; and in their own good time the other southern states in which Negro voters had constituted a serious problem did the same thing. Some reverses were experienced in the courts, but the net result of this epidemic of anti-Negro suffrage legislation was to eliminate for the time being all danger that Negro voters might play an important part in southern politics.

With this problem out of the way, or at least in process of solution, it became possible for the rural whites of the South to resume the struggle for a voice in public affairs that they had begun in the days of the Alliance and had continued under the banner of Populism. They did not form again a third party, but they did contest freely at the Democratic primaries against the respectable and conservative descendants of the "Bourbons." The Tillman machine in South Carolina continued to function smoothly for years as the agency through which the poorer classes sought to dominate the government of that state. It regularly sent Tillman to the United States Senate, where after his death his spirit lived on in the person of Cole Blease. In Georgia the struggle for supremacy between the two factions of the Democratic party was a chronic condition with now one side and now the other in control. Ex-Populists, converted by the lapse of time into regular organization Democrats, won high office and instituted many of the reforms for which they had formerly been defamed. Even Tom Watson rose from his political deathbed to show amazing strength in a race for Congress in 1918 and to win an astounding victory two years later when he sought a seat in the United States Senate. For better or for worse, the political careers of such southern politicians as James K. Vardaman of Mississippi, the Honorable Jeff Davis of Arkansas, and Huey P. Long of Louisiana demonstrate conclusively the fact that the lower classes in the South can and sometimes do place men of their own kind and choosing in high office. In these later days rural whites, who fought during Populist times with only such support as they could obtain from Republican sources, have sometimes been able to count as allies the mill operatives and their sympathizers in the factory districts; and southern primary elections are now apt to be as exciting as the regular elections are tame. Populism may have had something to do with the withdrawal of political power from the southern Negro, but it also paved the way for the political emancipation of the lower-class southern whites.

The control of the government by the people was for the thoughtful Populist merely a means to an end. The next step was to use the power of the government to check the iniquities of the plutocrats. The Populists at Omaha, when they were baffled by the insistence of the temperance forces, pointed out that before this or any other such reform could be accomplished they must "ask all men to first help us to determine whether we are to have a republic to administer." The inference is clear. Once permit the people really to rule, once insure that the men in office would not or could not betray the popular will, and such regulative measures as would right the wrongs from which the people suffered would quickly follow. The Populists believed implicitly in the ability of the people to frame and enforce the measures necessary to redeem themselves from the various sorts of oppression that were being visited upon them. They catalogued the evils in their platforms and suggested the specific remedies by which these evils were to be overcome.

Much unfair criticism has been leveled at the Populists because of the attitude they took toward the allied subjects of banking and currency. One would think from the contemporary anti-Populist dia-

tribes and from many subsequent criticisms of the Populist financial program that in such matters the third-party economists were little better than raving maniacs. As a matter of fact, the old-school Populists could think about as straight as their opponents. Their newspapers were well edited and the arguments therein presented usually held together. Populist literature, moreover, was widely and carefully read by the ordinary third-party voters, particularly by the western farmers, whose periods of enforced leisure gave them ample opportunity for reading and reflection. Old party debaters did not tackle lightly their Populist antagonists, and as frequently as not the bewhiskered rustic, turned orator, could present in support of his arguments an array of carefully sorted information that left his better-groomed opponent in a daze. The injection of the somewhat irrelevant silver issue considerably confused Populist thinking, but, even so, many of the "old-timers" kept their heads and put silver in its proper place.

The Populists observed with entire accuracy that the currency of the United States was both inadequate and inelastic. They criticized correctly the part played by the national banking system in currency matters as irresponsible and susceptible of manipulation in the interest of the creditor class. They demanded a stabilized dollar and they believed that it could be obtained if a national currency "safe, sound, and flexible" should be issued direct to the people by the government itself in such quantities as the reasonable demands of business should dictate. Silver and gold might be issued as well as paper, but the value of the dollar should come from the fiat of government and not from the "intrinsic worth" of the metal. It is interesting to note that since the time when Populists were condemned as lunatics for holding such views legislation has been adopted which, while by no means going the full length of a straight-out paper currency, does seek to accomplish precisely the ends that the Populists had in mind. Populist and free silver agitation forced economists to study the money question as they had never studied it before and ultimately led them to propose remedies that could run the gauntlet of public opinion and of Congress. The Aldrich-Vreeland Act of 1908 authorized an emergency currency of several hundred million dollars to be lent to banks on approved securities in times of financial disturbance. A National Monetary Commission, created at the same time, reported after four years' intensive study in favor of a return to the Hamiltonian system of a central bank of the United States; but Congress in 1914, under Wilson's leadership, adopted instead the Federal Reserve system. The Federal Reserve Act did not, indeed, destroy the national banks and avoid the intervention of bankers in all monetary matters; but it did make possible an adequate and elastic national currency varying in accordance with the needs of the country, and it placed supreme control of the nation's banking and credit resources into the hands of a Federal Reserve Board, appointed, not by the bankers, but by the president of the United States with the consent of the Senate. The Populist diagnosis had been accepted and the Populist prescription had not been wholly ignored.

Probably no item in the Populist creed received more thorough castigation at the hands of contemporaries than the demand for subtreasuries, or government

warehouses for the private storage of grain; but the subtreasury idea was not all bad, and perhaps the Populists would have done well had they pursued it farther than they did. The need that the subtreasury was designed to meet was very real. Lack of credit forced the farmer to sell his produce at the time of harvest when the price was lowest. A cash loan on his crop that would enable him to hold it until prices should rise was all that he asked. Prices might thus be stabilized; profits honestly earned by the farmers would no longer fall to the speculators. That the men who brought forward the subtreasury as a plan for obtaining short-term rural credits also loaded it with an unworkable plan for obtaining a flexible currency was unfortunate; but the fundamental principle of the bill has by no means been discredited. Indeed, the Warehouse Act of 1916 went far toward accomplishing the very thing the Populists demanded. Under it the United States department of agriculture was permitted to license warehousemen and authorize them to receive, weigh, and grade farm products, for which they might issue warehouse receipts as collateral. Thus the owner might borrow the money he needed; not, however, from the government of the United States.

In addition to the credits that the subtreasury would provide, Populist platforms usually urged also that the national government lend money on farm lands directly at a low rate of interest. This demand, which received at the time an infinite amount of condemnation and derision, has since been treated with much deference. If the government does not now print paper money to lend the farmer with his land as security, it nevertheless does stand back of an elaborate system of banks through which he may obtain the credit he needs. Under the terms of the Federal Reserve Act national banks may lend money on farm mortgages—a privilege not enjoyed in Populist times—and agricultural paper running as long as six months may be rediscounted by the Federal Reserve Banks. From the Farm Loan Banks, created by an act of 1916, the farmers may borrow for long periods sums not exceeding fifty per cent of the value of their land and twenty per cent of the value of their permanent improvements. Finally, through still another series of banks—the Federal Intermediate Credit Banks, established by an act of 1923—loans are made available to carry the farmer from one season to the next, or a little longer, should occasion demand; the intermediate banks were authorized to rediscount agricultural and livestock paper for periods of six months to three years. Thus the government has created a comprehensive system of rural credits through which the farmer may obtain short-term loans, loans of intermediate duration, or long-term loans, whichever his needs require, with the minimum of difficulty and at minimum interest rates. It would be idle to indulge in a *post hoc* argument to try to prove that all these developments were due to Populism; but the intensive study of agricultural problems that led ultimately to these measures did begin with the efforts of sound economists to answer the arguments of the Populists. And it is evident that in the end the economists conceded nearly every point for which the Populists had contended.

More recent attempts to solve the agricultural problem, while assuming the responsibility of the government in the matter as readily as even a Populist could have asked, have progressed beyond the old Populist panacea of easy credit. Agricultural economists now have their attention fixed upon the surplus as the root of the difficulty. In industry production can be curtailed to meet the demands of any given time and a glutted market with the attendant decline of prices can in a measure be forestalled. But in agriculture, where each farmer is a law unto himself and where crop yields must inevitably vary greatly from year to year, control of production is well-nigh impossible and a surplus may easily become chronic. Suggestions for relief therefore looked increasingly toward the disposal of this surplus to the greatest advantage. The various McNary-Haugen bills that came before Congress in recent years proposed to create a federal board through which the margin above domestic needs in years of plenty should be purchased and held or disposed of abroad at whatever price it would bring. Through an "equalization fee" the losses sustained by "dumping" the surplus in this fashion were to be charged back upon the producers benefited. This proposition, while agreeable to a majority of both houses of Congress, met opposition from two successive presidents, Coolidge and Hoover, and was finally set aside for another scheme, less "socialistic." In 1929 Congress passed and the president signed a law for the creation of an appointive Federal Farm Board whose duty it is, among other things, to encourage the organization of coöperative societies through which the farmers themselves may deal with the problem of the surplus. In case of necessity, however, the board may take the lead in the formation of stabilization corporations which under its strict supervision may buy up such seasonal or temporary surpluses as threaten to break the market and hold them for higher prices. A huge revolving fund, appropriated by Congress, is made available for the purpose, loans from this fund being obtainable by the stabilization corporations at low interest rates. There is much about this thoroughly respectable and conservative law that recalls the agrarian demands of the nineties. Indeed, the measure goes farther in the direction of government recognition and aid to the principle of agricultural coöperation than even the most erratic Allianceman could have dared to hope. Perhaps it will prove to be the "better plan" that the farmers called for in vain when the subtreasury was the best idea they could present.

To the middle-western Populist the railway problem was as important as any other—perhaps most important of all. Early Alliance platforms favored drastic governmental control of the various means of communication as the best possible remedy for the ills from which the people suffered, and the first Populist platform to be written called for government ownership and operation only in case "the most rigid, honest, and just national control and supervision" should fail to remove the "abuses now existing." Thereafter the Populists usually demanded government ownership; although it is clear enough from their state and local platforms and from the votes and actions of Populist officeholders that, pending the day when ownership should become a fact, regulation by state and nation must be made ever more effective. Possibly government ownership is no nearer today than in Populist times, but the first objective of the Populists, "the most rigid, honest and just national control," is as nearly an accomplished fact as carefully drawn legislation and highly

efficient administration can make it. Populist misgivings about governmental control arose from the knowledge that the Interstate Commerce Act of 1887, as well as most regulatory state legislation, was wholly ineffectual during the nineties; but beginning with the Elkins Act of 1903, which struck at the practice of granting rebates, a long series of really workable laws found its way upon the statute books. The Hepburn Act of 1906, the Mann-Elkins Act of 1910, and the Transportation Act of 1920, not to mention lesser laws, placed the Interstate Commerce Commission upon a high pinnacle of power. State laws, keeping abreast of the national program, supplemented national control with state control; and through one or the other agency most of the specific grievances of which the Populists had complained were removed. The arbitrary fixing of rates by the carriers, a commonplace in Populist times, is virtually unknown today. If discriminations still exist as between persons and places the Interstate Commerce Commission is likely to be as much to blame as the railroads. Free passes, so numerous in Populist times as to occasion the remark that the only people who did not have passes were those who could not afford to pay their own fare, have virtually ceased to exist, except for railway employees. Railway control of state governments, even in the old "Granger" states, where in earlier days party bosses took their orders direct from railway officials, has long since become a thing of the past. The railroads still may have an influence in politics, but the railroads do not rule. Governmental control of telephones, telegraphs, and pipe lines, together with such later developments as radio and the transmission of electric power, is accepted today as a matter of course, the issues being merely to what extent control should go and through what agencies it should be accomplished.

For the trust problem, as distinguished from the railroad problem, the Populists had no very definite solution. They agreed, however, that the power of government, state and national, should be used in such a way as to prevent "individuals or corporations fastening themselves, like vampires, on the people and sucking their substance." Antitrust laws received the earnest approval of Alliancemen and Populists and were often initiated by them. The failure of such laws to secure results was laid mainly at the door of the courts, and when Theodore Roosevelt in 1904 succeeded in securing an order from the United States Supreme Court dissolving the Northern Securities Company, it was hailed as a great victory for Populist principles. Many other incidental victories were won. Postal savings banks "for the safe deposit of the earnings of the people" encroached upon the special privileges of the bankers. An amendment to the national constitution in 1913, authorizing income taxes, recalled a decision of the Supreme Court that the Populists in their day had cited as the best evidence of the control of the government by the trusts; and income and inheritance taxes have ever since been levied. The reform of state and local taxation so as to exact a greater proportion of the taxes from the trusts and those who profit from them has also been freely undertaken. Labor demands, such as the right of labor to organize, the eight-hour day, limitation on the use of injunctions in labor disputes, and restrictions on immigration, were strongly championed by the Populists as fit measures for curbing the power of the trusts

and were presently treated with great consideration. The Clayton Antitrust Act and the Federal Trade Commission Act, passed during the Wilson régime, were the products of long experience with the trust problem. The manner in which these laws have been enforced, however, would seem to indicate that the destruction of the trusts, a common demand in Populist times, is no longer regarded as feasible and that by government control the interests of the people can best be conserved.

On the land question the Populist demands distinctly foreshadowed conservation. "The land," according to the Omaha declaration, "including all the natural resources of wealth, is the heritage of all the people and should not be monopolized for speculative purposes." Land and resources already given away were of course difficult to get back and the passing of the era of free lands could not be stopped by law; but President Roosevelt soon began to secure results in the way of the reclamation and irrigation of arid western lands, the enlargement and protection of the national forests, the improvement of internal waterways, and the withdrawal from entry of lands bearing mineral wealth such as coal, oil, and phosphates. At regular intervals since 1908 the governors of the states have met in conference to discuss the conservation problem, and this one-time dangerous Populist doctrine has now won all but universal acceptance.

It would thus appear that much of the Populist program has found favor in the eyes of later generations. Populist plans for altering the machinery of government with but few exceptions have been carried into effect. Referring to these belated victories of the Populists, William

Allen White—the same who had asked, "What's the matter with Kansas?"—wrote recently, "They abolished the established order completely and ushered in a new order." Thanks to this triumph of Populist principles, one may almost say that in so far as political devices can insure it, the people now rule. Political dishonesty has not altogether disappeared and the people may yet be betrayed by the men they elect to office, but on the whole the acts of government have come to reflect fairly clearly the will of the people. Efforts to assert this newly won power in such a way as to crush the economic supremacy of the predatory few have also been numerous and not wholly unsuccessful. The gigantic corporations of today, dwarfing into insignificance the trusts of yesterday, are in spite of their size far more circumspect in their conduct than their predecessors. If in the last analysis "big business" controls, it is because it has public opinion on its side, and not merely the party bosses.

To radicals of today, however, the Populist panaceas, based as they were on an essentially individualistic philosophy and designed merely to insure for every man his right to "get ahead" in the world, seem totally inadequate. These latter-day extremists point to the perennial reappearance of such problems as farm relief, unemployment, unfair taxation, and law evasion as evidence that the Populist type of reform is futile, that

something more drastic is required. Nor is their contention without point. It is reasonable to suppose that progressivism itself must progress; that the programs which would solve the problems of the one generation might fall far short of solving the problems of a succeeding generation. One may not agree with the contention of some present-day radicals that only a revolution will suffice, and that the very attempt to make existing institutions more tolerable is treason to any real progress, since by so doing the day of revolution may be postponed. But one must recognize that when the old Populist panaceas can receive the enthusiastic support of Hooverian Republicans and Alsmithian Democrats, their once startling reforms have passed from the left to the right and are no longer to be regarded as radical measures at all. One is reminded of the dilemma that Alice of Wonderland fame encountered when she went through the looking-glass. On and on she ran with the Red Queen, but "however fast they went they never seemed to pass anything."

"Well, in our country," said Alice, still panting a little, "you'd generally get to somewhere else—if you ran very fast for a long time, as we've been doing."

"A slow sort of country!" said the Queen. "Now, *here*, you see, it takes all the running *you* can do to keep in the same place. If you want to get somewhere else, you must run at least twice as fast as that!"

The interpretation that Progressivism originated in Populist demands was first questioned in the late 1940s by GEORGE E. MOWRY (1909–   ), ironically a doctoral student of Professor Hicks at the University of Wisconsin a decade earlier. Presently teaching at UCLA, Professor Mowry is a respected authority of the Progressive era by virtue of three excellent books. Unlike the differences between Chamberlain and Parrington, those between Mowry and his former teacher have little to do with ideology; evidence is at the center of this debate. What kinds of evidence did Mowry use to lay the groundwork for the thesis that now goes by the name of the "status revolution"? And if he is right, does this mean that Hicks was altogether wrong?*

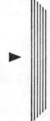

The Urban Gentry on the Defensive

Just what was a California progressive before he took office in 1910, and before power and the exigencies of politics altered his beliefs? What were the springs of his action, his personal aspirations, his concepts of what constituted the good society? Fortunately for the purpose of answering these important questions, the men who organized the California progressive movement were both literate and historically minded. The solid collections of personal manuscripts they so considerately left behind them, the diaries, documents, and innumerable published articles afford the historian an unrivaled opportunity in recent American history to inquire into the origins and the mentality of a grassroots movement. Moreover, the progressive group was small. Fewer than a hundred men attended the two state-wide progressive conferences held in Oakland in 1907 and 1909 before victory swelled the number of the organization's would-be leaders. Of this number the author has been able to track down biographical data on forty-seven men, data which produces a striking picture of similarity in background, economic base, and social attitudes, and which furthermore suggests

* Reprinted from *The California Progressives* by George E. Mowry with the permission of the publishers, University of California Press. © 1951 by the Regents of the University of California. Footnotes omitted by permission.

the strongly selective process inherent in such movements.

Compositely, the California progressive leader was a young man, often less than forty years old. He had probably been born in the Middle West, in Indiana, Illinois, Wisconsin, or Iowa. If not, then he was native to the state. He carried a north-European name, and unless he was one of the two notable exceptions, came of old American stock. These statistics of national origin are even more striking when cast upon the total character of California's polyglot and immigrant population in 1910.

The long religious hand of New England rested heavily upon California progressivism, as it has on so many American movements. Of the twenty-two progressives whose biographies indicate a religious affiliation, seven were Congregationalists, two were Unitarians, and four were Christian Scientists. The educational history of the League's leaders lends additional testimony to their social stratification. In a day when higher education was almost monopolized by the upper middle classes, three of every four had had a college education, and three of the group had studied in European universities. Occupationally, the California progressive held a significant niche in the American economic structure. In the sample obtained, there were seventeen attorneys, fourteen journalists, eleven independent businessmen and real-estate operators, three doctors, and three bankers. At least one-half of the journalists owned their own papers or worked for a family enterprise, and the lawyers, with two exceptions, were not practicing politicians. In the entire group, only two had any connection with a large industrial or financial corporation, save for the ownership of shares.

This was a group of highly literate, independent free enterprisers and professional men.

While not wealthy, the average California progressive was, in the jargon of his day, "well fixed." He was more often than not a Mason, and almost invariably a member of his town's chamber of commerce. Finally, he apparently had been, at least until 1900, a conservative Republican, satisfied with McKinley and his Republican predecessors.

Naturally, some fundamental questions arise about these fortunate sons of the upper middle class. Inheriting a secure place in society, earning a reasonably good living, and certainly not radical by temperament, what prompted their political revolt, and what did they want? The answers, of course, like those to most social questions, are extremely complex. They did not lie in California alone or even in the United States, for in its larger aspects the progressive movement was a western European phenomenon, its impulse being felt all over the Western world at the end of the nineteenth and beginning of the twentieth century. Wherever one found that characteristic ferment arising out of Western society's attempt to adjust its archaic agrarian social system to the new industrial and urban world, there one found the moral, humanitarian, and democratic strains of progressivism.

In the United States, what later came to be called the progressive movement started with the birth of the new century. Historically, it drew upon the farmer and labor protests of the preceding forty years, as well as upon the writings of the great nineteenth-century social critics. The Grangers and the Populists, Henry George, Edward Bellamy, and Henry Demarest Lloyd, along with the more strictly literary figures, all made their contributions to the national progressive mentality. But progressivism was not just a reformulation of an older radicalism. Late nineteenth-century tides of nationalism and social religion were also important in the evolution of its basic doctrines. On the whole, its leaders were drawn from a different class than were those of the Grangers and the Populists. In its origins it was an urban rather than a rural movement, and where it did touch the countryside it grew most spectacularly not in the Populist wheat, cotton, and mining regions, but rather in states with more diversified and wealthier economies.

In general, twentieth-century national progressivism was a protest by some peculiarly individualistic social and economic groups against the rapid concentration of twentieth-century American life and its attending ethical, economic, and political manifestations. Since the newly arisen giant business corporation was both the most conspicuous example and agent of that concentrating force, the national progressive attack was launched first against the monopolistic corporation, with its economic and political power and vast corruption of public life. At the same time, whether the average progressive realized it or not, the movement was essentially a protest against the changing group and individual relationships growing out of the new industrial and urban social complex. Largely an upper middle-class movement, at least in its leadership, progressivism was not opposed to private property but rather to the impersonal, concentrated, and supposedly privileged property represented by the behemoth corporation. Looking backward to an older America, it sought to recapture and

reaffirm the older individualistic values in all the strata of political, economic, and social life.

This great wave of political activity, starting in the United States about 1900, soon left its mark upon literature, journalism, education, and the church. The governments of great cities like Toledo, Cleveland, St. Louis, and Minneapolis felt its touch. Its philosophy became the aim of state governments when Robert La Follette was elected governor of Wisconsin in 1900 and Albert Cummins of Iowa in 1902. It invaded national politics when Theodore Roosevelt proclaimed it from the White House after 1901.

Since California progressivism developed relatively slowly, it was inspired and influenced by progressives and progressive achievements elsewhere. From 1906 to 1910, Robert La Follette, Joseph W. Folk, Albert B. Cummins, Ray Stannard Baker, and Gifford Pinchot, all spoke in the state in behalf of the progressive cause. Throughout the early progressive campaigns in California, Folk's St. Louis and La Follette's Wisconsin were cited repeatedly as a city and a state that had freed themselves from the old iniquitous politics. But of all the outside personal forces operating to inspire progressive rebellion in California, Theodore Roosevelt was by far the greatest. His name and his doctrines were grafted into the very origins of the movement, and his position in national affairs was repeatedly used by the Californians as an effective answer to the charges of party treason raised against them. But Theodore Roosevelt was not venerated simply for the advantage his position afforded them. To a great degree, the President's moral and political doctrines struck close to the California progressive ideal. He was a source of inspiration, a symbol of progressive virtues, and a protector at the highest court.

The California progressive did not need to search outside the state, however, for the crude social materials that resulted in the progressive mind. By 1900 California was essentially a microcosm generating all the conditions that led to the progressive ferment elsewhere. Many of the social forces necessary for the progressive revolt, in fact, were far more advanced inside the commonwealth than they were in the Middle Western states of its origin. Perhaps nowhere in the nation was the life of the state dominated to such a degree by one corporation as was California by the Southern Pacific Railroad. What the Standard Oil trust was to the United States in the 'eighties, the Southern Pacific was to California in 1900—and more. Few other states were as urban as California where almost 50 per cent of its population lived in four metropolitan districts. That meant a large upper middle class of old American stock, composed of persons not too far removed from the attitudes of the individualistic Middle West. Labor, moreover, was organized in the San Francisco region as it was in few other places in the nation. There, as in open-shop Los Angeles, violent class conflict raged, expressing itself through the San Francisco Union Labor party, the bombing of the *Times* in Los Angeles, the state-wide rise of the Socialist party, the Southern Pacific's political machine, and the employers' organizations dedicated to destroying unionism.

When the younger representatives of the upper middle class in California became aware of these conflicting, organized class forces, progressivism was born.

It is clear that the California progressive reacted politically when he felt himself hemmed in, and his place in society threatened by the monopolistic corporation on the one side, and by organized labor and socialism on the other. Proof for this general conclusion is not hard to find. The earliest manifestation of what later became progressivism in California is apparent in two local movements which started in 1906, one aimed against the Southern Pacific political machine in Los Angeles, and the other against the control of the Union Labor party in San Francisco. In the opening speech of the progressive crusade against the Southern Pacific in Los Angeles, Marshall Stimson voiced a fundamental principle. The three choices which confronted the voters of the city, he said, were between, "a government controlled by corporate interests, Socialism, or if we have the courage, unselfishness and determination, a government of individuals."

Although Rudolph Spreckels felt it necessary, in launching the graft investigation in San Francisco, to declare that this was not "a class question" between capital and labor but one "of dishonesty and justice," his very phraseology indicated that there was a third group interested in civic affairs with different public standards from those of either labor or capital. From that time until victory in 1910, progressive literature was critical both of politically organized capital and politically organized labor.

The progressive revolt was not only, or perhaps even primarily, a matter of economics. A few progressives had been hurt economically by the railroad and other semimonopolistic corporations; certainly shippers and farmers had been. But the progressive leaders were mainly editors, attorneys, small businessmen, and real-estate operators. Instead of beggaring these men, the railroad occasionally subsidized them, as Fremont Older pointed out. Moreover, this was not a period of depression: mass immigration into the state and the resulting spiral in real-estate values, the great oil boom, the coming of the movies, and the expansion of fruit and vegetable farming produced a wave of prosperity in California which lasted until 1913. If the progressive leaders saw a real and immediate threat from the large corporation to their own economic stake in society, it is not apparent from their letters and their speeches. Nowhere did the California progressives suggest that the big corporation be abolished.

Not quite so much can be said of their attitude toward the labor union. Admitting in theory that the union was a necessary organization in the modern industrial world, the progressives' bias against labor was always greater than against the large corporation. Even the more radical progressives hoped that unions were only a "temporary expedient representing the necessity of one class standing against another" until the time the country got "beyond the questions of class and caste." Most progressives felt that unions could do very little economically for the working man. "The law of supply and demand," Chester Rowell observed, "applies to wages as well as to other prices." In the long run there was "no escaping" that law. Even where unions had demonstrably raised wages for their members, the progressives were sure that the benefits applied only to the few and really hurt the many. Unionism was "but a war measure to provide relative justice to a few." Many progressives could not see why the skilled laborer needed the union for economic

purposes, since they considered him the "American aristocrat," who "got the highest wages . . . fixed his own terms . . . and constituted our only leisure class."

So long as organized labor was reasonably ineffective as an economic bargaining agent, the California progressives were inclined to view the movement more or less tolerantly. But as soon as labor aspired to a closed shop, Chester Rowell inveighed against this goal as "antisocial, dangerous, and intrinsically wrong." When the Johnson administration later considered a limitation to the issuance of labor injunctions, Meyer Lissner bitterly protested that if labor's legal status was changed the closed shop would soon be upon Los Angeles as it had been in San Francisco. Lissner was ready, he wrote to Governor Johnson, to let their entire reform movement go down the drain "rather than let Los Angeles be thrown under the sort of tyrannical domination of labor unionism that exists in San Francisco."

The progressive's prejudice against organized labor is further indicated by the fact that not one progressive leader was recruited from the ranks of the unions. In the midst of an early fight against the Southern Pacific machine in Los Angeles, Meyer Lissner wrote that while it was all right "to work through the labor unions" and get their support, he was against any publicity of the tactics. "It may react," he added. Lissner's attitude in 1908 contrasts strongly with his willingness three years later to coöperate with anyone, including the remnants of the old Southern Pacific machine in the city, to stop the challenge of the Socialist party, supported by organized labor.

Despite the attitudes of the Los Angeles group, the progressive opposition to labor on economic grounds should not be overestimated. In the north, Fremont Older, Rudolph Spreckels, Francis Heney, William Kent, and Hiram Johnson were all supporters of labor unions even though they did attack the corrupt Union Labor party. Johnson had acted as counsel for several San Francisco unions, and for years Older's paper had been frankly prolabor. Both Kent and Heney felt that a large part of their political support came from the laboring ranks, and Heney remarked that it was wiser to trust the labor vote "to stand for what is right and decent in government" than it was to trust the businessmen. Returning from a vacation, Rudolph Spreckels found that the directors of his bank had voted to give $20,000 to the open-shop fund of the San Francisco Chamber of Commerce. Spreckels risked his presidency to fight the action and succeeded only after two antilabor directors had resigned. With Chester Rowell and Irving Martin, editor of the Stockton *Record,* he went to labor's defense repeatedly when industry organized to break the unions and create an open-shop economy.

If there is some evidence to suggest that the progressive orientation against labor was partly economic in origin, what explains the progressive opposition to the Southern Pacific Railroad and its associated corporations? Disgruntlement with insufficient political rewards may have activated some of the older progressive leaders, who, according to Senator Works, had previously worn "the collar of the railroad without seeming irritation." And undoubtedly some of the younger men who later became progressives were incensed when their youthful and independent political efforts were defeated by the machine. But to ascribe the later reform zeal of this minor group

to these early defeats begs the larger question. Why did so many young progressives originally engage in independent politics and why, when once spanked, did they not learn their lesson as so many generations of young men had before them, and either quit the game or make their peace with the machine? The answer does not lie entirely in the realm of immediate self-interest but in the broader reaches of human intellect, emotion, and group psychology. Squarely to the point is the fact of the opposition of many progressives, including some of the very rich, not only to the privileged corporations but also to great wealth, particularly if it had been accumulated by means they considered unsocial. As most of them later distinguished between "good" and "bad" trusts, so did they distinguish between "good" and "bad" wealth. Like a repentant sinner, William Kent opened his congressional campaign in 1910 with an apology for his wealth accumulated by land speculation and with a promise to use his fortune to wipe out the system by which he had accumulated it. Few, if any, progressives would have agreed with the novelist Boyensen that all efforts to achieve great wealth were a denial of beauty. But many of them did believe with Goldsmith that:

Ill fares the land to hastening ills a prey
Where wealth accumulates and men decay.

"Modern politics," Henry Adams wrote in *The Education of Henry Adams,* "is a struggle not of men but of forces. The men become every year more and more creatures of force massed about central power houses." With the struggle for power between capital and labor penetrating almost every level of California life, and with the individual more and more ignored, the California progressive was increasingly sensitive to that drift and increasingly determined to stop it if possible. This was obvious in his obsession, with the nightmare of class consciousness and class rule. "Class government is always bad government," the progressive Los Angeles *Express* vehemently declared, and added that unions "have no more right to usurp the management of public affairs than have the public service corporations." Chester Rowell, probably the most literate of the California progressives, went on to gloss that statement. "Class prejudice among the businessmen," he wrote, "excuses bribery and sanctifies lawlessness and disorder among labor. When the spectre of class rule is raised, then all questions of truth, right, and policy disappear, and the contest is no longer over what shall be the government but wholly who shall be it." This class spirit on both sides, the editor of the Fresno *Republican* lamented, "is destroying American liberty." When it became predominant, he predicted, American institutions would have to be changed. "For upon that evil day reform ends and nothing but revolution is possible."

Clearly what troubled the independent progressive about both organized capital and labor was not only economics, but questions of high politics, group prestige, group morality, and group power. Involved also was the rising threat to an old American way of life which he represented and which he considered good.

The progressive was a member of an old group in America. As businessman, successful farmer, professional man or politician, he had engaged in extremely individualistic pursuits and had, since the decline of the colonial aristocracy, supplied most of the nation's intellectual, moral, and political leadership. Still confident that he possessed most of society's virtues, the California progressive was acutely aware in 1905 that many of society's rewards and badges of merit were going elsewhere. Before the days of the Rotarians and kindred organizations, he was excluded from or did not care to join the Union League Club or the union labor hall. Although well-educated, he was all but excluded from politics unless he accepted either corporate or labor domination, a thing he was exceedingly loath to do. His church, his personal morality, and his concept of law, he felt, were demeaned by the crude power struggle between capital and labor.

On the defensive for the first time since the disappearance of the old aristocracy, this class of supreme individualists developed a group consciousness themselves. Although generally overlooked by the historian, this consciousness had already developed in some farming elements in the Populist period. Nothing else can be concluded from the words of the official organ of the Michigan State Farmers' Alliance. "It has been truly said," remarked that paper, "that the People's Party is the logical and only nucleus for every element of the American population that stands for social stability and constitutional rights. It is the bulwark against anarchy of the upper and lower scum of society."

Now in the twentieth century, flanked by organized labor on one side and organized capital on the other, the urban California progressives took up that song. Their letters, journals, and speeches are full of the phrases, "our crowd," "the better element," and "the good people of the state." Even their political enemies recognized their separateness as indicated by the names they conferred upon them. The phrases "goo-goo" and "Our

Set" dripped with ridicule. But they also indicated awareness of the progressives' claim to ethical and political superiority. A clear expression of the progressive's self-confidence in his own moral elevation and his contempt for other classes can be found in an editorial of the progressive organ, the *California Weekly*. "Nearly all the problems which vex society," this illuminating item ran, "have their sources above or below the middle-class man. From above come the problems of predatory wealth.... From below come the problems of poverty and of pigheaded and brutish criminality." Notwithstanding the average progressive's extreme individualism, this statement was unmistakably an expression of a social group on the march.

The California progressive, then, was militantly opposed to class control and class consciousness when it emanated either from below or above him. This was his point of opposition. What was his positive creed? In the first place this "rank individualist," as he gladly styled himself, was in most cases an extremely religious man. His mind was freighted with problems of morality, his talk shot through with biblical allusions. He often thought of the political movement he had started as a part of the "Religion Forward Movement." As early as 1903, A. J. Pillsbury, who was later to become a leading progressive, praised Theodore Roosevelt for coming nearer "to exemplifying the New England conscience in government than any other president in recent times."

But if the religion of the California progressive was old American in its form, much of its content was a product of his recent past. Gone was the stern God of the Puritan, the abiding sense of tragedy and the inherent evilness of man. As William Allen White later wrote, the cult of the hour was "to believe in the essential nobility of man and the wisdom of God." With an Emersonian optimism, the California progressive believed that evil perished and good would triumph. Sin may have been original, but it did not necessarily have to be transmittable. There was "no natural compulsion," William Kent wrote, "including the lust for blood, the savage passion for reproduction, and the cruder forms of theft that ought not to be overcome by education and public opinion." Under the influence of Darwinism, the rising social sciences, and a seemingly benign world, the progressive had traded some of his old mystical religion for a new social faith. He was aware that evil still existed, but he believed it a man-made thing and upon earth. What man created he could also destroy, and his present sinful state was the result of his conditioning. An editorial in Fremont Older's San Francisco *Bulletin* expressed this reasoning: "The basic idea behind this age of liberalism is the simple one that all men, prisoners and free, rich and poor, are basically alike in spirit. The difference usually lies in what happens to them." And from that one could conclude that when men were given justice, they would return justice to society. The progressive, then, not only wanted to abolish a supernatural hell; he was intent upon secularizing heaven.

There were, of course, individual variations from these generalized patterns. Chester Rowell, for one, while agreeing that men should not be treated as free moral agents, protested against considering them as "mere creatures of environment." "If we try to cure the trouble by curing the environment," Rowell argued, "we shall never go far enough, for however much we protect men from temptation there will be some left and men will fall to that. . . . Dealing with society the task is to amend the system. But dealing with the individual man the task is to reiterate forever, 'thou shall not steal' and tolerate no exceptions. . . ." But Rowell was more of a child of his age than even he realized. Despite his strictures on the sinfulness of man, one found him writing later that Taft's peace treaties made international war impossible because "the moral influence on nations [for peace] would be tantamount to compulsion."

"The way to have a golden age," one progressive novelist wrote, "is to elect it by an Australian ballot." This was an extreme affirmation of democracy, but it followed logically from the progressive belief in the fundamental goodness of the individual. To a surprising degree, this fervent belief in the "rightness" of the democratic process separated the progressive from the conservative politician who usually insisted upon a "representative government" and held that "pure democracy" was a dangerous thing. A few progressives, like Rudolph Spreckels, Chester Rowell, and Senator Works had serious doubts about the efficacy of absolute democracy. For most of them, however, democracy was a thing to venerate.

According to progressive thought, behind every political question was a moral question whose answer "could safely be sought in the moral law." Since most men were ethical agents, public opinion was the final distillate of moral law. It was a jury that "could not be fixed," observed Lincoln Steffens, and to some progressives, it was "God moving among men." For this reason C. D. Willard objected to Theodore Roosevelt's characterization of democracy as just a means to

an end. To Willard, democracy was a positive moral force in operation, a good in itself. "It is," he wrote, "a soul-satisfying thing."

Back in the 1890's, Senator Ingalls of Kansas had remarked, "The purification of politics is an iridescent dream." Dream or not, that was one of the major goals of the California progressive a decade later. There was but one law for him—that of the church-going middle class—and he was convinced that it should be applied equally to the home, to government, and occasionally even to business. It was in this spirit that Hiram Johnson admonished his followers to forget how to make men richer and concentrate on how to make them better. This attitude helps to explain much of the progressive interest in sumptuary legislation. Individualism was a sacred thing as long as it was moral individualism; otherwise it needed to be corrected. Thus the progressive proposals for the abolition of prize fighting ("a form of social debauchery"), gambling, slang ("since it is a coverup for profanity"), prostitution, and the liquor traffic. And thus his demands for the censorship of literature, the drama, and social dancing.

In protest against these "holier-than-thou-people" among his fellow progressives, C. K. McClatchey, owner of the Sacramento *Bee,* wrote that he was his "brother's keeper only in so far as I should set him a good example. . . ." And though the progressive, on the whole, vehemently denied the full import of this statement when applied to morality, generally he was not in complete disagreement with McClatchey's views when they were applied to economics. Good Christian that he was, and on the whole benevolent, the California progressive did not quarrel with the doctrine of wardship, provided it was not pushed too far. He stood ready in 1910 to protect obviously handicapped individuals and he was ready and even eager to eradicate what he called "special privilege," which to his mind fundamentally limited opportunity for the man on the bottom to make his way economically upward. A few individuals on the left of the movement, like Congressman William Kent, felt that the progressive and socialist movements were "only different phases of the same tendency" and that soon property rights were going "to tumble about the heads of the men" who had built themselves "pyramids of money in a desert of want and suffering." And Fremont Older raised the disturbing question of why men should be paid fortunes who were lucky enough to have been born with brains or in fortunate environments. One might as well go back to the feudal system, Older answered himself, because there was no more personal merit "in having talent than in having a noble lineage."

But for the most part, the progressive was content with the basic concepts of the economic system under which 1910 capitalism awarded its profits and its pains. He firmly believed in private property, profits, and especially the competitive system and even acknowledged that the corporation and the labor union were necessary instruments of modern business. What the progressive did object to in the year of his triumph was not 1910 capitalism as such, but rather the ideological, economic, moral, and political manifestations which had arisen from that system. He was confident, at least in 1910, that no inevitable causal relation existed between that system and its social results. Moreover, he felt sure that

the nexus between the great corporations and the government, on the one hand, and organized labor and government, on the other, could be broken. Once those links were destroyed, he was certain that most of the political corruption would vanish; once "special privilege" was removed, the system would right itself and the individual again would be supreme in economics as well as in politics.

"I would not be a dredger Congressman, or a farm Congressman, or a fresh egg Congressman, or a dairy Congressman," William Kent assured the voters of his district in which all those pursuits flourished. "I would like to be an American Congressman, recognizing the union and the nation." This denial of economic representation and the emphasis upon the general welfare is a perfect example of what the progressive politico saw in himself. Subjectively, he pictured himself as a complete individual wholly divorced from particular economic as well as class interests. Ready to do justice in the name of morality and the common good, he was, in his own estimation, something akin to Plato's guardians, above and beyond the reach of corrupting material forces.

California progressivism was an expression of an older America objecting to the ideological and social drifts of the twentieth century. Representing a particular strain of middle-class individualism, the progressive became militant when he felt himself hemmed in between the battening corporation and the rising labor unions. Considering himself the solid moral element in America, he became exceedingly group conscious even though his group was a collection of supreme individualists. His was a psychological group as well as an economic one, and his rising sensitivity was due as much to social, moral, and political causes as it was to the economic factor. If one can generalize on admittedly shaky grounds, his opposition to the corporation was more political and psychological in nature than it was economic, while perhaps the reverse was true of his attitude toward organized labor. The progressive end—a classless state—was also one of the ends of the Marxists; the difference lay in the kind of classlessness. Whereas the communist, after a violent political and economic revolution, would have frozen his state on the proletariat level, the progressive thought it possible to achieve and perpetuate a middle-class, capitalist level through the peaceful political instrument of democracy. Unlike the Marxists, the California progressives believed it possible to stop the rise of class loyalties without removing existing economic inequalities or destroying existing economic groups. Since he thought primarily in political terms, his main concern was to remove class consciousness from politics. "Progressivism," Chester Rowell wrote in 1912, "believes in nationalism, in individual citizenship, and in the whole people, not in any class as a unit of government. It opposes class government by either the business, the laboring, or any other class, and resists the formation of class parties. It is, in other words, the twentieth-century evolution of democracy."

The California progressive, then, wanted to preserve the fundamental patterns of twentieth-century industrial society at the same time that he sought to blot out, not only the rising clash of economic groups but the groups themselves, as conscious economic and political entities. But he sought to do all this, at least before he had actually taken power, without profound economic re-

form. "The people," Rowell observed sometime after the progressive victory in 1910, "elected Governor Johnson to get moral and political reform." The word "economic" was significantly absent from the statement. From today's vantage point, the progressive's aim of a capitalist commonwealth:

Where none were for a class and all were for the state,
Where the rich man helped the poor and the poor man loved the great,

may seem incredibly naïve. His stress on individualism in a maturing industrial economy was perhaps basically archaic. His refusal or inability to see the connection between economic institutions and the rising class consciousness indicated a severe case of social myopia. His hopes to avert class strife by political and moral reform alone were scarcely realistic. And paradoxical in the extreme was the coexistence of his own intense group loyalties with his strong antipathy to the class consciousness of organized capital and organized labor.

When the California progressive confidently took control of the state in 1910, the road ahead was uncertain indeed. What, for example, would happen to the fundamental beliefs of this group if they found their ends could not be achieved without substantial economic reform; if in spite of their efforts, labor threatened their economic and political estate; if many of them became economically and psychologically absorbed in the advancing corporate system; if in a less prosperous age than 1910, the clash between economic groups for a livelihood created intense social friction? Would their moral calculus, their spirit of benevolence, their faith in men, their reverence for democracy still persist?

The fate of progressivism and perhaps the fate of democracy in the twentieth century were wrapped up in the answers to those questions. For between militantly organized and class-conscious capital and equally militant class-conscious labor, the progressive represented for California a makeweight for compromise, a pivot on which the democratic process could swing. California urgently needed that makeweight in 1910, until the state and the nation could reconcile the contending ambitions of capital and labor on a better basis than dynamite and the general strike, and company police and the lockout. Time was needed to relax the taut emotions of men, time and just enough action to lull the social pangs of the economic groups below, and not frighten the wealthy groups above.

Whether or not the progressive could fulfill this role of skillful broker depended not only on his intelligence but also on his heart and ethical sense. Whether he realized it or not, he was himself a capitalist and belonged to one of society's more fortunate groups. In trying to modify the struggle between organized capital and labor, he would be faced in the long run with the necessity of giving up some of his own social perquisites as well as some of the social power of his class. William Kent, for one, believed that it could be done. During the 1910 campaign he wrote an open letter to the working people of his congressional district maintaining, "While the inspiration has always come from below in the advance of human rights . . ." the final accomplishments had come from "the disinterested work of men who, having abundant means, have ranged themselves on the side of those most needing help." A year later he went on to gloss that statement. "I don't believe in the class struggle," he said, "because while the impulse must come from the underdog, every great reform has been taken up and worked out by those who are not selfishly interested. I believe altruism is a bigger force in the world than selfishness." In the largest sense, the rock of progressivism was to rest upon this faith. Whether it was true, and to what degree, only the years following the progressive victory could tell.

Not until this decade was the popular status-revolution thesis of the 1950s challenged. Born in New Jersey, educated at Rutgers and Harvard, and currently teaching at Georgetown University, J. JOSEPH HUTHMACHER (1929–   ) has written about the ethnic basis of politics in the East. His first book was an important study of the Yankee-Irish cleavage in Massachusetts. At present he is working on a biography of Senator Robert F. Wagner of New York City's Tammany Hall. In the following article Professor Huthmacher criticizes the Mowry school for ignoring the creative role of the non-Anglo-Saxon urban masses in the Progressive era.*

The Urban Masses on the Move

Most historians of twentieth-century America would agree that the effective beginnings of the present-day "people's capitalism"—the present-day liberalism—can be traced back to the Progressive Era. And most of them would agree that the essential ingredient which made possible the practical achievement of reforms at that time was the support given by city dwellers who, at the turn of the century, swung behind reform movements in large numbers for the first time since America's rush into industrialism following the Civil War. True, the Populists and other agrarian radicals had done spade-work on behalf of various proposals in the late nineteenth century, such as trust regulation, the income tax, and direct election of senators. But their efforts had gone unrewarded, or had been frustrated by enactment of half-way measures. Not until the reform spirit had seized large numbers of urbanites could there be hope of achieving meaningful political, economic, and social adjustments to the demands of the new industrial civilization.

Between 1900 and 1920 American statute books became studded with the results of urban-oriented reform drives.

* J. Joseph Huthmacher, "Urban Liberalism and the Age of Reform," *Mississippi Valley Historical Review*, XLIX (September 1962), 231–241. Reprinted with the permission of the Mississippi Valley Historical Association and the author.

The direct primary, the initiative, the Seventeenth Amendment; the Clayton Act, a revived Interstate Commerce Commission, and the Federal Trade Commission; workmen's compensation, child labor laws, and Prohibition—these and many other achievements testified to the intensity of Progressivism. It is admitted, of course, that not everything done in the name of reform was desirable. Some measures, notably Prohibition, are counted today as being wrong-headed, while some political panaceas like the direct primary elicited an undue degree of optimism on the part of their exponents. Nevertheless, the Progressive Era did witness America's first modern reform upsurge, and much of substantial worth was accomplished. Moreover, it established patterns and precedents for the further evolution of American liberalism, an evolution whose later milestones would bear the markings "New Deal" and "New Frontier."

In accounting for the genesis and success of urban liberalism in the Progressive Era, however, the historians who have dominated its study thus far have concentrated on one population element, the urban middle class, and its Yankee-Protestant system of values. "The great majority of the reformers came from the 'solid middle class,'" Professor George E. Mowry tells us. "If names mean anything, an overwhelming proportion of this reform group came from old American stock with British origins consistently indicated." Professor Richard Hofstadter adds that "the key words of Progessivism were terms like *patriotism, citizen, democracy, law, character, conscience* . . . terms redolent of the sturdy Protestant Anglo-Saxon moral and intellectual roots of the Progressive upris-

ing."[1] The component parts of this amorphous middle class, and the reasons for their new interest in reform at the turn of the century, have been described by various scholars.[2] We have been told about the "white collar" group which saw, in the increasing bureaucratization of big business, the blotting out of its traditional belief in the American "rags to riches" legend. Some writers have dwelt upon the middle-class intellectuals —writers, publicists, ministers, college women, professors—who, in response to changing patterns of social thought represented by the rise of "realism" in literature, religion, and the social sciences, determined to uplift the living conditions of their less fortunate brothers. Others have examined the "Old Aristocracy" threatened by a "status revolution," and fighting to maintain the degree of deference that had been theirs before the rise of the newly rich moguls of business and finance.

Imbued with this mixture of selfish and altruistic motives, reinforced by the pocketbook-pinching price inflation that got under way in 1897, the urban middle-class reformers set out to right the wrongs of their society. They introduced a variety of new democratic techniques into our political mechanics, in an attempt to break the grip of the corrupt bosses who manipulated irresponsible immigrant voters and unscrupulous busi-

[1] George E. Mowry, *The Era of Theodore Roosevelt, 1900-1912* (New York, 1958), 86; Richard Hofstadter, *The Age of Reform* (New York, 1955), 318.

[2] Mowry, *Era of Theodore Roosevelt*; Hofstadter, *Age of Reform*; C. Wright Mills, *White Collar* (New York, 1951); Eric Goldman, *Rendezvous with Destiny* (New York, 1952); Samuel P. Hays, *The Response to Industrialism, 1885-1914* (Chicago, 1957).

nessmen in ways that subverted good government. They augmented the government's role as watchdog over the economy, either to maintain the traditional "small business" regime of competitive free enterprise, or at least to make sure that oligopolists passed on to consumers the benefits of large-scale operation. Through the activities of their philanthropic organizations, coupled with support of paternalistic labor and social welfare legislation, the middle-class reformers also sought to uplift the standards of the alien, slum-dwelling, urban working class to something more closely approximating the Yankee-Protestant ideal. So runs the "middle-class" interpretation of Progressivism, an interpretation which has set the fashion, by and large, for scholarly work on the subject.

There is no doubt, of course, that discontented elements among the urban middle class contributed much to Progressivism, or that the historians who have explored their contributions and their motives deserve the plaudits of the profession. Nevertheless, it may be pertinent to ask whether these historians have not overstressed the role of middle-class reformers, to the neglect or exclusion of other elements—such as organized labor—who have had something to do with the course of modern American liberalism.[3] More particularly, a number of circumstances call into question the assertion that "In politics . . . the immigrant was usually at odds with the reform aspira-

tions of the American Progressive."[4] If such were the case, how does one explain the drive and success of Progressive Era reform movements in places like New York and Massachusetts—states that were heavily populated with non-Protestant, non-Anglo-Saxon immigrants and sons of immigrants? How could reformers succeed at the polls or in the legislatures in such states if, "Together with the native conservative and the politically indifferent, the immigrants formed a potent mass that limited the range and the achievements of Progressivism"?[5] Moreover, how does one explain the support which individuals like Al Smith, Robert F. Wagner, James A. Foley, James Michael Curley, and David I. Walsh gave to a large variety of so-called Progressive measures in their respective office-holding capacity?[6] Surely these men do not conform to the middle-class, Yankee-

[3] The suggestions made in this and the following paragraphs stem primarily from the author's research for *Massachusetts People and Politics, 1919-1933* (Cambridge, Mass., 1959), and for a projected biography of Senator Robert F. Wagner of New York. Senator Wagner's papers are deposited at Georgetown University, Washington, D.C.

[4] Hofstadter, *Age of Reform,* 180-81. It is clear, of course, that Professor Hofstadter is referring not only to the first-generation immigrants themselves, but to the whole society which they, their offspring, and their culture were creating within our industrial, urban maze.

[5] *Ibid.,* 181.

[6] Oscar Handlin, *Al Smith and His America* (Boston, 1958); Joseph F. Dinneen, *The Purple Shamrock: The Honorable James Michael Curley of Boston* (New York, 1949); Dorothy G. Wayman, *David I. Walsh: Citizen Patriot* (Milwaukee, 1952). See also Arthur Mann, *La Guardia: A Fighter against His Times* (Philadelphia, 1959). Among the measures which Robert F. Wagner introduced as a New York state senator between 1909 and 1918 were the following: a bill to provide for direct election of United States senators; a bill to authorize a twenty million dollar bond issue for conservation and public development of state water power; a direct primary bill; a short-ballot bill; a resolution to ratify the federal income tax amendment; a bill establishing the Factory Investigating Commission; a civil rights bill; a woman suffrage amendment to the state constitution; numerous bills for child labor regulation; a bill to extend home rule to municipalities; a bill to establish a minimum wage commission

Protestant "Progressive Profile" as etched by Professor Mowry.[7]

If the Progressive Era is to be considered a manifestation of the Yankee-Protestant ethos almost exclusively, how does one explain the fact that in the legislatures of New York and Massachusetts many reform bills received more uniform and consistent support from representatives of the urban lower class than they received from the urban middle-class or rural representatives? Some of the most effective middle-class reformers, such as social worker Frances Perkins, realized this fact at the time and charted their legislative strategy accordingly.[8] It may be pointed out also that, even when submitted to popular referendums, typically Progressive measures sometimes received more overwhelming support in the melting-pot wards than they received in the middle-class or rural constituencies. This was the case, for example, in Massachusetts when, in 1918, the voters passed upon a proposed initiative and referendum amendment to the state constitution. Such circumstances become especially compelling when we remember that reform measures, no matter how well formulated and publicized by intellectuals, cannot become effective in a democracy without skillful political generalship and—even more important—votes.

Marshaled together, then, the foregoing evidence suggests that the triumphs of modern liberalism in the Progressive Era, and in subsequent reform eras, were owed to something more than a strictly middle-class dynamism. It indicates that the urban lower class provided an active, numerically strong, and politically necessary force for reform—and that this class was perhaps as important in determining the course of American liberalism as the urban middle class, about which so much has been written.

Today's liberals look to the "northern" Democrats and the "eastern" Republicans—those whose elections are due largely to the votes of the urban working class—for support of their proposals. If, as is contended, this phenomenon of urban lower-class liberalism can be traced back beyond the election of 1960, beyond the New Deal, and to the Progressive Era, then the probing of its chronological origins and the operational details of its emergence present wide fields for fruitful research. In the process of such studies, many other questions will present themselves to the investigator. What were the sources of lower-class interest in reform? How did its sources affect its nature, specific content, and practical effects? How, if at all, did urban lower-class liberalism differ in these respects from urban middle-class liberalism? At the risk of premature generalization, tentative suggestions, indicated by research thus far conducted, may be set forth regarding these matters.

The great source of urban working-class liberalism was experience. Unlike the middle-class reformers, who generally relied on muckrakers, Social Gospelers, and social scientists to delineate the ills of society, the urban working class knew at first hand the conditions of life on "the other side of the tracks." Its members and spokesmen grew to manhood "in the midst of alternately shivering and sweltering humanity in ancient rat-infested rookeries in the swarming,

for women; a bill limiting the issuance of labor injunctions; a bill to authorize municipal ownership of power plants; and a corrupt practices bill.

[7] Mowry, *Era of Theodore Roosevelt*, chap. 5.

[8] Frances Perkins, *The Roosevelt I Knew* (New York, 1946), 12–26.

anonymous, polyglot East Side, an international center before the U.N. was
dreamed of," where "souls and bodies
were saved by the parish priest, the
family doctor, and the local political
saloonkeeper and boss who knew everyone and was the link between the ex-
ploited immigrant and the incompre-
hensible, distant law."[9] Such people
were less imbued than the middle class
with the "old American creed" which
expounded individualism, competition,
and laissez-faire free enterprise as the
means of advance from "rags to riches."
Their felt needs, largely of the bread
and butter type, were of the here and
now, and not of the middle-class variety
which fastened upon further advancement to a higher station from one already fairly comfortable. Moreover, their
constant immersion in the depths of
human misery and frailty, and the semi-
pessimistic nature of their religious psychology, limited their hopes for environmental improvement within the bounds
of reasonable expectation. Their outlook
tended to be more practical and "possi-
bilistic" than that of some middle-class
Progressives who allowed their reform
aspirations to soar to Utopian heights,
envisaging a "Kingdom of God on
Earth" or a perfect society to be achieved
by means of sociological test tubes. Finally, the previous political experience
of the immigrant workers, centering
about their security-oriented relations
with a paternalistic ward boss, condi-
tioned them to transfer the same func-
tional conception to the city, state, and
national governments as they became
progressively aware of their ability,
through their voting power, to make
those governing bodies serve their needs.

Consequently, their view of government
was much less permeated with fears of
paternalism and centralization than that
of traditionally individualistic middle-
class reformers, many of whom abated
their attachment to the laissez-faire principle with only the greatest trepidation.[10]

The influence of these conditioning
factors seems clearly discernible in the
specific types of reform programs to
which the urban lower class and its
spokesmen lent greatest support. It is
commonplace to say, for example, that
the immigrants were not interested in
political machinery reforms simply as
reforms. Unlike the remaining middle-
class "genteel reformers," they did not
look upon political tinkering as the be-
all and end-all of reform. Yet it is an
injustice to imply that the immigrants'
attitude on this matter was due to an
inherent inability to comprehend the
Yankee-Protestant concept of political
behavior, and that they were therefore
immune to all proposals for political
reform. These lower-class voters seemed
willing enough to support specific proposals which would enable them to secure the voice necessary to satisfy their
economic and social needs, recognizing,
quite properly, that the latter were the
real sources of society's maladjustment.
Since the rural areas of Massachusetts
generally controlled the Bay State legislature, the urban working class supported the initiative and referendum
amendment which might enable them
to by-pass tight-fisted rural solons. Since
the same situation prevailed in the New
York legislature, the New York City dele-
gation was glad to secure popular election of United States senators. In brief,
it would seem that the line-up on such
questions depended more upon local con-

9 Robert Moses, "Salute to an East Side Boy Named Smith," *New York Times Magazine* (October 8, 1961), 113.

10 See Hofstadter, *Age of Reform,* chap. 6.

ditions of practical politics than upon the workings of a Yankee-Protestant ethos.

In the realm of economic reform, pertaining particularly to the problem of "big business," indications are that the urban lower class tended—unwittingly, of course—to favor the "New Nationalism" approach of Herbert Croly and Theodore Roosevelt over the "New Freedom" of Wilson and the trust-busters. Its members had seldom experienced the white collar group's "office boy to bank president" phenomenon themselves. They had never been part of the "Old Aristocracy," and hence had not suffered a downward revision in status at the hands of big business moguls. They shared few of the aspirations of the industrial "small businessman" and, indeed, recognized that the latter was all too frequently identified with sweatshop conditions. Consequently, the urban lower class was little stirred by Wilsonian cries to give the "pygmies" a chance. To workers the relative size of the employer's establishment was quite immaterial so long as he provided job security and adequate wages and working conditions, and passed some of the benefits of large-scale production on to consumers in the form of lower prices. Governmental stabilization of the economy and regulation of big business might well prove more successful in guaranteeing these conditions than would government antitrust drives. As a result, we find urban lower-class representatives introducing a large variety of business regulatory measures on the local and state levels during the Progressive Era. And it is symbolic, perhaps, to find Senator Robert F. Wagner introducing the National Industrial Recovery Act in 1933, while Senator David I. Walsh of Massachusetts had sponsored somewhat similar, forerunner,

measures in Congress during the 1920's.

What has been said above indicates the basis for urban lower-class interest in the many types of social welfare and labor measures which became novelties, and then commonplace enactments, during the Progressive Era. If the middle class faced the fear of insecurity of status, then the working class faced an equally compelling fear of insecurity of livelihood and living conditions. The precarious condition of the lower class had now become known even to those on the better side of the tracks and, partly for humanitarian reasons and partly to defend their own civilization against a "revolution from below," middle-class reformers had become interested in social justice movements—which involved "doing things for others." But the recipients of this benevolence might surely be expected to show at least an equal interest in such movements—which involved doing something for themselves. That such was the case is clearly indicated by study of the legislative history of measures like workmen's compensation, widows' pensions, wages and hours legislation, factory safety legislation, and tenement laws in the legislatures of New York and Massachusetts during the Progressive years. The representatives of lower-class constituencies were the most active legislative sponsors and backers of such bills and, in collaboration with middle-class propagandists and lobbyists, they achieved a record of enactments which embraced much of the best and most enduring part of the Progressive Era's heritage.

The operations of the New York State Factory Investigating Commission are a case in point. Established by the legislature following the tragic Triangle Shirtwaist Company fire in 1911, the Commission recommended and secured passage of over fifty labor laws during the next four years, providing a model factory code that was widely copied in other states. The Commission's most active legislative members were State Senator Robert F. Wagner and Assemblyman Alfred E. Smith, two products of the East Side, while its most effective investigator and lobbyist was Miss Frances Perkins, a middle-class, college trained social worker. (It should be noted also that the Commission received notable assistance from Samuel Gompers and other leaders of organized labor.) Again it is rather striking to observe that the Social Security Act of 1935, which began the transfer of industrial security matters from the state to the national level, was introduced by Senator Wagner, to be administered by a federal Department of Labor headed by Miss Perkins.

Effective social reform during the Progressive Era, and in later periods, seems thus to have depended upon constructive collaboration, on specific issues, between reformers from both the urban lower class and the urban middle class (with the further co-operation, at times, of organized labor). Of course, such co-operation could not be attained on all proposals that went under the name of social "reform." When, during the Progressive Era, certain old-stock, Protestant, middle-class reformers decided that the cure for social evils lay not only in environmental reforms, but necessitated also a forcible "uplifting" of the lower-class immigrants' cultural and behavior standards to "100 per cent American" levels, the parting of the ways came. Lower-class reform spokesmen had no use for compulsory "Americanization" through Prohibition, the closing of parochial schools, or the enforcement of puritanical "blue laws." Nor had they any use for immigration restriction laws which were based upon invidious, quasi-racist distinctions between allegedly "superior" and "inferior" nationality stocks.[11] To them reform, in so far as the use of government compulsion was concerned, was a matter of environment. The fundamentals of a man's cultural luggage—his religion, his emotional attachment to his "old country" and its customs, his habits and personal behavior —were of concern to himself and his God, and to them alone. The lower-class reformers were products of the melting pot, and most of them took seriously the inscription on the base of the famous statue in New York harbor. True, there were many religious and ethnic differences among the component elements of the lower class, which often resulted in prejudice and violence. But each of these elements resented the Old Stock's contention that all of them were equally inferior to the "real Americans" of Yankee-Protestant heritage, and they resisted the attempts, which grew as the Progressive Era wore on, to enforce conformity to a single cultural norm.

In so far as conformity-seeking "cultural" reforms were enacted in the Progressive years, then, the responsibility must be assigned to urban middle-class reformers, joined in this instance by their rural "bible belt" brethren. The lower class can share no part of the "credit" for reforms like Prohibition. But in resisting such movements, were they not waging an early fight on behalf of what

11 "If the literacy test was not applied to the Irish and the German, why should it now be applied to the Jew, the Italian or the Slav of the new immigration? Like our ancestors, they are now flying from persecution, from ignorance, from inequality; like our ancestors they expect to find here freedom and equal oportunity. Are we going to deny them an equal opportunity? Are we going to withhold from them the equality and opportunities which our fathers enjoyed?" (Excerpt from a speech by Robert F. Wagner in the New York State Senate, on a resolution which he introduced in 1917 petitioning Congress not to pass the literacy test bill. Wagner Papers).

we today call "cultural pluralism"—acceptance of which has become a cardinal tenet in the standard definition of "liberalism" in the modern world? Indeed, it may not be too much to say that in all three fields of reform—the political and economic, as well as the social—indications are that the urban lower-class approach was more uniformly "advanced" than that of the middle class, in the sense of being more in line with what has become the predominant liberal faith in modern America. After all, does not the lower-class reform impulse, as outlined above, resemble the "hard-headed," realistic, and pluralistic liberalism for which spokesmen like Reinhold Niebuhr and Arthur Schlesinger, Jr., plead today, so that the "Children of Light" might not fall easy prey to the "Children of Darkness"? [12]

It is not contended, of course, that all members of the urban working class became interested in reform during the Progressive Era, any more than it can be contended that all members of the urban middle class did so. The same "sidewalks of New York" that produced Al Smith and Robert Wagner continued to produce their share of "unreconstructed" machine politicians, whose vision never rose above their own pockets. Nor is it argued that the nature and zeal of lower-class attachment to liberalism remained constant throughout the twentieth century, or that the degree of co-operation attained with other reform minded elements remained unchanging. In the 1920's, for example, mutual suspicion and distrust, based largely on ethnic or "cultural" differences, seem to have displaced the former mood of limited collaboration between lower- and middle-

class spokesmen, and in these changed circumstances Progressive-type measures found little chance of enactment. It is also possible that the high level of general prosperity prevailing since 1941 has vitiated urban working-class devotion to economic reform, and that the increasing degree of acceptance enjoyed by ethnic elements formerly discriminated against is causing their members to forget the lessons of cultural pluralism. All of these matters deserve further study.

The last-mentioned problems, dealing with the contemporary scene, may lie more properly within the realm of the political scientist and sociologist. But surely the evolution of America's twentieth-century liberal society, from the Progressive Era through the New Deal, is a province for historical inquiry. It is suggested that the historians who enter it might do better if they modify the "middle-class" emphasis which has come to dominate the field and devote more attention to exploring hitherto neglected elements of the American social structure. Such exploration necessitates tedious research, focusing at first on the local and state levels, in unalluring source materials such as local and foreign-language newspapers, out-of-the-way manuscript collections, and the correlations between the make-up and voting records of small-scale election districts. In the course of this research, however, our conception of the Progressive Era, and of recent American history as a whole, may undergo change. In fact, it may even begin to appear that "old fashioned" political historians, if they inform their work with up-to-date statistical and social science skills, still have as much to contribute to our knowledge of ourselves as do the intellectual and social historians, who are, perhaps, sometimes prone to over-generalize on the basis of historical psychoanalysis.

[12] See, for example, Reinhold Niebuhr, *The Children of Light and the Children of Darkness* (New York, 1945); Arthur M. Schlesinger, Jr., *The Vital Center* (Boston, 1949).

Social justice was a Progressive goal, and no one needed
it more than the immigrants of the slums subjected to
economic hardship and nativist abuse. How did the
Progressives react to these new Americans? Pretty
decently, answers JOHN HIGHAM (1920–   ) in
the piece below. They welcomed the newcomers,
appreciated their Old World customs, and rejected the
prejudice that would shortly result in restrictive
legislation. A native of Queens, New York City,
Professor Higham teaches intellectual history at the
University of Michigan. His *Strangers in the Land,*
awarded a Dunning Prize in 1956, is the standard study
of bigotry in the United States between 1860 and 1925.*

A Brake on Nativism

William Allen White remarked that
discontent had shaved its whiskers,
washed its shirt, and put on a derby. His
comment described a movement that had
little need of nativism.

Many progressives, to be sure, were
troubled by the increasing magnitude of
immigration. A few of them espoused
the cause of organized labor and shared
its feeling that the newcomers threatened
both the unions and the living standards
they were fighting for. A larger number,
especially progressives from rural and
small-town backgrounds, deeply dis-
trusted the big city. In that center of

moral pestilence, alien settlement now
concentrated more exclusively than ever
before. The almost complete identification of the immigrant with his urban
environment prevented a sympathetic response toward either on the part of many
reformers. Furthermore, a strain of elit-
ism made some progressive intellectuals
contemptuous of malingerers on the highway of progress. The sociologist Edward
A. Ross, one of the most nativistic of
progressives, defined democracy as government by talent, not by the "narrow,
short-sighted, muddle-headed . . . average
man." His Wisconsin colleague John R.

* Reprinted from John Higham, *Strangers in the Land.* Atheneum, 1963. Copyright
1955, 1963 by Rutgers, the State University. Reprinted by permission of Rutgers University
Press.

Commons opened an influential book on immigration by taking issue with the equalitarian assumptions of the Declaration of Independence.

Divided though it was on ethnic issues, progressive sentiment on balance probably weighed against nativism in the halcyon years before 1910. In addition to its self-assurance, the movement as a whole radiated the equalitarian idealism that Ross and Commons thought unrealistic. Compared with previous middle-class reformers, progressives drew from the hopeful atmosphere of the early twentieth century a larger confidence in the capacity of ordinary people to set things aright if given the means to do so. Believing ardently in the people, they sometimes included the immigrants in that category. They located evil primarily in the economic environment, and when they did so consistently they could respond to the immigrant as an innocent victim of bad conditions. The *Arena,* a liberal journal which had quaked at the foreign peril in earlier years, now accused nativists of blaming immigrants for the failures of America's own economic institutions. And when Mr. Dooley, the comic sage of Progressive America, heard that foreigners don't assimilate, he replied that America's digestion had gone wrong from too much rich food: ". . . if we'd lave off thryin' to digest Rockyfellar an' thry a simple diet like Schwartzmeister, we wudden't feel th' effects iv our vittels," declared Mr. Dooley.

No part of the progressive movement sloughed off its former xenophobia more thoroughly than did the campaign against municipal corruption. Unlike previous civic reformers, progressives uncovered connections between urban bosses and the business interests they protected. The foreign-born voter ceased to bear the brunt of the blame for misgovernment. Lincoln Steffens' pioneering exposé, *The Shame of the Cities,* held American business responsible and dismissed talk about the foreign vote as hypocritical. Frederic C. Howe made the same shocked discovery after starting in Cleveland politics with an exactly opposite impression. Throughout the 1900's, the National Municipal League paid virtually no attention to the immigrant until its president, Charles J. Bonaparte, happily informed the members that "the admirable assimilative processes of our orderly freedom are turning out Americans with as much facility as Dickens' sausage factory, which was capable of turning paving-stones into sausages."

An economic interpretation of political problems could not dispel all concern at how the immigrants cast their votes, but legislation could end the more flagrant scandals. The Naturalization Act of 1906 finally terminated the wholesale distribution of citizenship papers on the eve of elections. Under easygoing Jeffersonian legislation that had lasted more than a century, as many as five thousand separate state courts were administering naturalization with no central supervision whatever. Corruption had flourished for decades. In addition to the thousands of immigrants naturalized for voting purposes on the eve of elections, many others secured bogus American citizenship papers in order to return to their native lands exempt from a subject's duties. Partly in response to State Department protests, the reform measure in 1906 restricted naturalization to certain courts, laid down a standardized procedure for them to follow, and established a federal Division of Naturalization to supervise the whole process. The law ignored entirely the old nativist demand for lengthening the residence requirement for citizenship. It aimed not at disfranchising the immigrant but at ending the conditions under which his vote was sold. It succeeded brilliantly and in doing so completed the separation between nativism and municipal reform.

Yet confidence was far from devotion. The progressives of the early twentieth century were unafraid, but in general they were also indifferent and aloof. Like the rest of their generation, they felt little enmity toward the immigrants but little identification with them either. A social and ideological gulf yawned between the well-established groups afire with visions of change and the uprooted folk who had already experienced more change than they could comprehend. The progressives seldom understood the strangers as fellow men with special problems of adjustment. They could be tolerant enough; they could often accept the old ideal of America's cosmopolitan nationality. But they could not believe that the newcomers might be significantly influencing American culture; at least they could not think so and retain their equanimity. Most native-born progressives in the early years of the century viewed the immigrant as a passive entity, malleable and still to be molded under the influences of American society. He was, in Charles Bonaparte's metaphor, sausage-meat. In beings so passive and remote the ordinary progressive took no great interest.

The logic of democracy, however, pointed beyond this negative tolerance. It pointed to a respect for the integrity and importance of all people, toward a cooperative concern with the problems of every group. Most progressives, while convinced of the solvent power of democracy, applied it largely to political and economic inequalities. That it might reform relationships among men of vary-ing creeds or colors or cultures did not impress them. On the other hand, some progressives glimpsed an ampler democratic vision. In addition to nativists like Ross and a larger group that was indifferent to ethnic issues, the progressive movement produced a small number of democratic humanists. In the cities a few early twentieth century liberals came into close enough contact with the immigrants to see them whole, to learn that poverty and isolation afflicted them in special ways, and to realize that democracy involved a social dimension which was unfulfilled as long as America simply took its foreign peoples for granted.

The beginnings lay in the social settlements. These had appeared in the slums of New York, Chicago, and other cities in the 1890's in response to the same rift between classes that aroused the nativists. Whereas the nativists struggled for social unity through hatred, the young men and women who moved into settlement houses hoped to bridge the class gulf through love. They went beyond traditional humanitarianism in two respects: in wanting to work with the people of the slums as well as for them, and in wanting to learn from them as well as teach them. Since the poorest sections of the cities were the foreign quarters, most of the people with whom settlement dwellers worked were immigrants. The democratic, experimental philosophy behind the settlements contrasted sharply with the nativistic tendencies of most late nineteenth century humanitarians and reformers. Of all old-stock Americans, settlement workers gained the fullest understanding, compassion, and respect for the new immigration.

Under the impact of the progressive movement, the settlements' attitude toward the foreign-born gradually spread to the ranks of professional social workers. Until the end of the nineteenth century, social work had been largely synonymous with charity, and for the most part its practitioners had loudly bewailed the immigrant flood that was swamping their resources. But now a philosophy of alleviation was giving way to one of prevention and social action. Welfare agencies, like municipal reformers and progressives generally, were discovering economic roots to the problems they faced. Instead of attributing poverty to moral weakness or to "hereditary pauperism," social workers turned toward the environment and toward its reconstruction. Some of the leading settlements were becoming veritable nurseries of reform, and as social workers fell into line they too saw the immigrants not as an oppressive burden but as an oppressed minority. In 1904 the organ of the New York Charity Organization Society shifted from hostility to unqualified sympathy for the foreign-born, and the National Conference of Charities made the same transition more gradually during the decade. After 1910 very few social workers who had intimate contact with foreign groups favored a further restriction of immigration.

Although the professional servants of society rallied behind a generous admission policy, their primary concern was with the treatment which the immigrants received after arrival. What needed reforming was the neglect and exploitation of the newcomers. They deserved educational opportunities to reduce their special handicaps and their special isolation; they should have protection from both Americans and their own fellow countrymen who took advantage of them. Combating indifference as much as nativism, social workers in the latter part of the progressive period planted the seeds of a public welfare program directed specifically at immigrant needs. This program flowered, however, under other influences and deserves a fuller discussion in a later context.

Along with a positive interest in the immigrants' welfare came a sense of their positive value to America—not just as hewers of wood and drawers of water, but as enriching additions to the whole culture. The traditional theory of America's cosmopolitan nationality emphasized the triumph of unity over diversity. Although the country was supposed somehow to gain from the blending process, no one had pointed proudly to the immigrants' concrete contributions to the final amalgam. The few progressive groups who actually worked with foreigners moved a step beyond the usual conception of assimilation.

Here again the settlements pioneered, because they respected foreign customs and approached the foreigners' problems in an empirical way. Experience soon taught a sensitive settlement founder like Jane Addams that the prevailing American contempt for the immigrant's past snarled his adjustment to the new environment. She saw particularly that a ruthless American chauvinism often infected the children of the immigrants, turning them against their parents and exposing them to the worst in their new surroundings. Experimentally, Jane Addams discovered that the settlements could check family disorganization by extending an appreciative welcome to Old World heritages. Several settlements began in the nineties to develop programs for conserving and celebrating the holidays, customs, folksongs, and languages of the nationalities in the neighborhood. In encouraging the newcomers to preserve the "best" in their own traditions, settlement leaders argued that each immigrant group had a tangible contribution to make to the building of American culture. Miss Addams and others came to believe that a more genuinely cosmopolitan society might emerge out of the mingling of old and new.

Originally a means of enhancing the foreigners' self-respect, the doctrine of "immigrant gifts" soon turned into a defense of the foreign-born from nativist attack and a justification for reform efforts in their behalf. The settlement people disseminated the doctrine widely after 1900, urging the general public as well as other social workers to appreciate the cultural contributions the strangers might make to American life. Allied reform elements absorbed the idea. The community center movement, which began about 1910 as an extension of the settlement ideal of unifying the jangling groups in urban areas, quickly appropriated the belief that America would gain by giving the immigrants greater opportunity to express their own inherent values. The chairman of the California State Commission of Immigration and Housing adopted a similar point of view, and New York's Governor Charles Evans Hughes was one of the early political leaders to praise the foreigners' contribution to American life.

A measure of these broader sympathies was passed along from the secular advocates of social welfare to the exponents of the Social Gospel, now the commanding force in American Protestantism. In the nineteenth century Josiah Strong and other Protestant reformers had regarded the foreign-born as a national menace, and the Protestant churches generally had shown too plain a hostility toward immigrants to take much thought for their religious or material welfare. Now the major denominations, moving more serenely on the currents of reform, developed a general interest in the strangers as fellow men—and as potential Protestants. The tasks of assimilating and evangelizing immigrants became linked to the whole religious attack on social problems. Although many churchmen could not entirely shed their fear and distrust, at least some Social-Gospelers adopted the "contributions" theory of assimilation. . . .

Thus the widening human sympathies of the progressive era called forth a new version of the cosmopolitan ideal of American nationality—a version emphasizing cultural accretion rather than racial blending. Undoubtedly the concept of immigrant gifts lent a certain status and dignity to the foreigner qua foreigner. Yet none of the progressives carried the idea very far; it represented a modification of the melting-pot tradition rather than a break from it.

One could talk in generalities about immigrant gifts far more easily than define them. No one even tried to discriminate what was "best" in the immigrants' past and worth preserving, from what might be bad or worthless. When examples of specific gifts came to mind, they turned out invariably to be things to which Americans attached slight importance: folk dances, music, exotic dishes, handicrafts, perhaps certain literary fragments. The contributions that charmed sympathetic progressives had no bearing on American institutions or ideals. A pageant prepared for Fourth of July celebrations expressed the gifts idea neatly. In this solemn drama immigrant groups in native costumes performed their national folk dances in an "offertory spirit" before a white-robed figure of America. It was all very genteel and uplifting, and very far removed from the rough, sweaty, painful adjustments that converted Europeans into Americans.

In the following excerpt from *The Uprooted,* a 1951 Pulitzer Prize history of immigration, OSCAR HANDLIN (1915–   ) arrives at conclusions different from Professor Higham's. Where the Michigan historian sees sensitivity, good will, and understanding, the Harvard historian observes callousness, hostility, and ignorance. But they are not looking at the same thing. Higham's thesis is about Progressive *social workers,* while Handlin's is about the Progressive *program* to destroy the immigrant-based political machine. Is it possible that both men are right, and that the Progressive era contains ambivalent attitudes toward race, nationality, and religion? Born in Brooklyn of immigrant parents, Professor Handlin has been the leading historian of American immigration for twenty-odd years.*

▶ A Wall of Misunderstanding

It was not surprising that the boss should see in the stirring of reform interests a threat to his own position. But it was significant that the mass of immigrants should regard the efforts of the various progressives with marked disfavor. In part this disapproval was based on the peasant's inherited distrust of radicalism; but it was strengthened by a lack of understanding among the radicals that deprived them of all influence among the newcomers. . . .

The division persisted down through the end of the century. The failure of socialists and anarchists to win an impor-

tant position in the associational life of the immigrants prevented them also from using these groups for political ends. And with few exceptions—Henry George for a time was one—American radicals met the stubborn opposition of the foreign-born voters. The populists made no headway at all in districts where the newcomers were numerous, and William Jennings Bryan could not hold the loyalty of such traditionally Democratic groups as the Irish.

The crisis came toward the close of the century, and in the first decade after, with the gradual formulation at many hands of a newer progressivism. Among the men involved in these movements there was certainly no trace of the wild-eyed reformer of the 1840's. Whether they fell in the camp of Theodore Roosevelt or Robert La Follette or any of the other figures who spoke for the trend, they were not at all inclined to tear apart and reconstruct the whole society. Yet their doctrines failed also to attract the immigrants.

To begin with, the movement lacked channels for communicating with the foreign-born citizens. There were among the progressives enough members of the second generation to have done so. But these, by the nature of the case, were the children of the immigrants who had broken with their parents' communities, who through education or personal advancement had moved away from the old beliefs and the old societies. They did not identify themselves with any group and therefore commanded the confidence of none.

On the other hand the reformers often found themselves in the position of attacking the recognized immigrant leaders. There was always the temptation to rely upon the tactics of exposure, to show up the corruption and venality of politicians; and there was often also an inclination to make clear the antecedents of those exposed. To blame the poor government of American cities on their immigrant residents was indeed calculated to win the favor of the native-born. But it drove the foreign-born to defend the boss as one of their own. In fact the reformer acquired the reputation of an informer, one who tattled and spitefully revealed the peccadilloes of essentially good men.

This attitude the progressives could

not understand. *The immigrant* (one among them complained) *lacks the faculty of abstraction. He thinks not of the welfare of the community but only of himself.* It never occurred to this critic that precious little thought was given by others to the welfare of the newcomers. If they did not consider their own interests, no one else would.

Certainly few among the reformers ever paused to consider what were the needs and interests of a new citizen or ever tried to imagine what such a one would have thought of their own confident remedies to the world's ills. The whole pack of innovations in the structure of government seemed to the foreign-born to be either mere tinkering or some subtle plot to steal control by undermining the familiar ways of political action. There was not likely to be much immigrant support for the initiative, referendum, and similar proposals.

The controversies over trusts and the regulation of business were also remote. Such issues excited the entrepreneur and the farmer; they had no immediate relevance to the life of the industrial worker. Debates about restraint of trade and railroad rates went on in a realm that did not directly concern him. He could only judge the attitudes of the reformers when they narrowed down to questions that had a direct bearing on his own mode of existence. And it was precisely on such questions that the reformers were farthest from him in point of view.

The problems of American municipalities had long troubled many men involved in the progressive movements. If innovations were slow to be introduced on a national scale, perhaps they could more easily be put into practice locally. Reform administrations had actually held office in some cities; and people could examine not only their professions but also their practices. Both alienated large numbers of immigrants.

There had been a mockery in the old boss's voice as he thought of the mistakes of his opponents: *I never saw a man in my life who made economy his watchword who was not always defeated before the people.* What did they promise, those fine folk who came gingerly into the district just before the election? They pledged themselves to lower taxes to voters who had no property to be taxed. They talked of balanced budgets and improved administration. Efficiency. System. Apply business methods to government.

As the score mounted up against them, they complained about corruption, ascribed their failure to the stuffed ballot box. Well, often enough the "floater" did come in to mark the paid-for crosses, and "repeaters" did move from precinct to precinct. But the reformers never understood it was they themselves had earned defeat, never realized that the most of the people they addressed did not want government to be a business. Efficiency too often expressed itself in an inhuman disregard for the individual; and system too often meant an unbending application of impersonal rules. A progressive administration often was one that laid off men to balance the budget. To the immigrants, the abstract principle was not worth the suffering it entailed. The boss knew that, as the reformers did not. Ultimately he was always the victor.

Yet among the new political currents that disturbed the closing years of the nineteenth century and the opening years of the twentieth there were some that also drew in the boss and through him a large part of his following. For many leaders it became increasingly difficult to operate on the old familiar personal level. There came a time in their careers when it was hard to apply the customary techniques. It was difficult to keep up with the new people who moved in; there were occasional lapses in recognition before the flow of hailing faces. With more applicants than places, each appointment made one friend and a half-dozen enemies. There was a strain, which grew heavier with the years, to the apportionment of favors.

Of course, there were no voluntary retirements. No one dropped the reins of power simply because the tug was too severe. The chief came as ever to the office and drove the best course he could. But often he wished there were some way to generalize the favors he dealt out. Or was it beyond the range of possibility that he should ever have for all his followers rewards, and never a denial?

The boss had not himself been forward in holding office. He had no wish for the prestige, knew well where the real power lay, and preferred to let someone else bear the responsibility. But the men who did become mayors and aldermen or governors and legislators shared his uneasiness about the burdens of control. In addition, some among them, without any thought of disputing his authority, nevertheless had vague ambitions that somehow they might make a name for themselves by helping those who had elected them.

A shrewd politician then could also observe the slow accumulation of potential voting strength around a new nucleus, the labor organization. The rising craft unions, mostly already affiliated with the American Federation of Labor, were

rather unfriendly to the unskilled immigrant workers. Yet among their members were many of the second generation,
linked through associational ties with the
boss and his machine; and the advantages
of an alliance came frequently to the
minds of both political and labor leaders.

The unions could hardly overlook the
possibilities of such support in their
struggle for recognition and position. In
the building trades, municipal ordinances
and inspection could be powerful weap-
ons, properly controlled. Any striker
knew the value of having the police on
his side. In the bitter warfare with in-
transigent employers, labor, like capital,
had sometimes summoned force to its aid.
In a few cases, the hired racketeers had
actually taken over, assumed the real
leadership of the unions; and these men
often, through their interest in gambling
and other illegal enterprises, already had
connections with the machine. In other
cases, the emergence of city-wide councils
or labor assemblies created agencies
through which an understanding could
be reached. This connection with labor,
together with the will of the boss to
generalize his favors and the aspirations
of the officeholders, combined to direct
immigrant political activity into new
channels.

It came out differently at the hands
of various men. For this was not the
application to practice of an idea already
understood, but the gradual working toward an idea from practices that circumstances dictated. Often corrupt alliances
with the underworld and the familiar
peanut politics mingled incongruously
with the newer procedures; and often
those who acted did not themselves understand the nature of their actions.

Back in 1892 John Peter Altgeld had
become Governor of Illinois. Himself an
immigrant, he had been put in office by
the Irish and Germans, to whom he had
pledged himself to protect the Catholic
and Lutheran parochial schools. His
connections led to Chicago, to the boss
Mike McDonald, to the gambler Joe
Martin, to the carpenter George Schill-
ing of the old eight-hour-day association.
Just after the turn of the century in San
Francisco, Eugene Schmitz and Abe Ruef
had come to power with the aid of the
Union Labor Party. A little later in
Eastern state legislatures the representatives of the city machines were making
themselves heard with uncommon vigor
—such men as Al Smith in New York
or David I. Walsh in Massachusetts or
Joe Tumulty in New Jersey.

There was not then even a program
to the specific measures they sponsored.
It may have been a law to force the
companies to sell five-cent cakes of ice,
or one to compel factory owners to install
safety devices, or one to limit the hours
of women. But there was not much certainty as to the theoretical grounds on
which they rested. A few of the Catholics among these politicians had heard
of the social encyclicals of Leo XIII; a
few Germans knew of the developments
in the Fatherland; a few Jews were thinking of an American equivalent for their
tradition of charity. But the measures
they furthered stemmed from more specific roots. These proposals were responses of men who, for a variety of
motives, remembered their own antec-
dents. When the thoughts came back of
the hot tenement room, of the pinned-up
sleeve where the crushed arm had been,
of the muffled sobs through the wall
where the weary mother could not rest,
then there welled up a painful recollec-
tion of the desperate needs that had once
engulfed them. Yes, even as they leaned

comfortably back, with their shining shoes on the oak desk, some chance glimpse through the window would bring to mind the urgency with which strangers, alone in a new and hostile world, had longed for security.

The machine that opened to the immigrants the prospect that the State might be the means through which the beginnings of security could come thereby assured itself of their loyalty. It also opened up the possibility of a very limited and very tentative collaboration with the reformers. The latter were still wrapped up in a kind of liberal thinking that refused to acknowledge that government could play a positive, directing role in society. Yet the progressives were also responsive to the appeal of humanitarian sentiments and, as they entered the second decade of the twentieth century, now and then they confronted measures that seemed undeniably good, however troubling they might be to laissez-faire assumptions. On workmen's compensation, factory and wage legislation there was room for an unrecognized accord between boss and "do-gooder."

The alliance had not yet become deliberate. A brief opportunity passed in the years when Woodrow Wilson became the spokesman of the reform impulse. As Governor and President he had received the credit for a number of enactments that seemed to help the laboring man; and his wartime nationalities policy had drawn the support of many immigrants by then interested in the fate of their old homelands. On the other hand, a number of influential groups came to hold him responsible for the "betrayal of Versailles"—the Irish, who saw in the League an instrument to secure the power of Great Britain; the Germans, dismayed by the vindictive terms of the Peace; and the Italians, disappointed at the boundary settlements.

As important perhaps was the fact that Wilson had never really broken through the limitations of the traditional reformer. In New Jersey he had disloyally quarreled with the machine that had elected him and had devoted much of his energy to tinkering with the forms of government. And as President he was sometimes insensitive to the particular desires of substantial groups in his following.

In any case, the era of Wilson led only to the era of normalcy. The reform tide ebbed. At the same time the likelihood of new legislation that might advance the security of the working people also receded, as the dominant political trend in the 1920's rejected any state interference in economic matters. In that decade the hold of the bosses on their following was stronger than ever.

Later, after the gates were closed and newcomers were no longer welcome, after a great collapse had shaken the confidence of other Americans, the surviving immigrants would find fresh hope that government might concern itself with their security. They would find this concern one of the various meanings of the New Deal; and their loyalty would not then be divided by the necessity of choosing between their own machines and reform. At that later time, the import of reform had changed so that it could swallow up their machines, bosses and all.

ARTHUR M. SCHLESINGER, JR. (1917–   ), special assistant to President John F. Kennedy and former Harvard history professor, has succeeded Vernon L. Parrington as the most widely-read liberal interpreter of American reform. Here, in a selection from the first volume of his still unfinished but already celebrated *Age of Roosevelt*, the historian of the New Deal portrays Progressivism as a precursor to the liberalism of the 1930s in its emphasis on the positive role that government should play in the economy. The student, in anticipation of Richard Hofstadter's interpretation that comes next, should note, too, how Schlesinger minimizes the differences between Woodrow Wilson and Theodore Roosevelt.*

 ► ## The New Freedom Fulfills the New Nationalism

The New Nationalism

[Theodore] Roosevelt transfixed the imagination of the American middle class as did no other figure of the time. With his squeaky voice, his gleaming teeth, his overpowering grin, and his incurable delight in self-dramatization, he brought everything he touched to life. His capacity for moral indignation was unlimited; his energy cascaded everywhere. He gathered into himself the mounting discontent with which Americans were contemplating business rule. By offering this discontent release in melodrama, he no doubt reduced the

pressure behind it for accomplishment. La Follette and others complained of his "rhetorical radicalism." His cannonading back and forth, La Follette said, filled the air with noise and smoke, but, when the battle cloud drifted by, little had been achieved. Yet Roosevelt's personality gave the reform movement a momentum it could hardly have obtained from economics alone. He stirred the conscience of America. Young men followed him in the service of the commonweal as they had followed no American since Lincoln.

Theodore Roosevelt, indeed, was more

complicated than he sometimes seemed. He sensed with brilliant insight the implications of America's new industrial might. At home, the industrial triumph had rendered acute the problems of economic justice and social peace. Abroad, it was thrusting America irrevocably into world power politics. With all the boisterousness of his personality, Roosevelt sought to awaken the nation to a recognition of new responsibilities. And the only way these responsibilities—domestic or foreign—could be met, he deeply believed, was by establishing a "powerful National government" and thus affirming national purpose as the guiding force in public policy.

Ancestry and outlook equipped Roosevelt peculiarly for this revival of a sense of national purpose. Coming from a well-born family in New York, inheriting wealth and independence, he considered himself above class allegiances. In particular, he looked with disdain on the business community. "I do not dislike," he wrote, "but I certainly have no especial respect or admiration for and no trust in, the typical big moneyed men of my country. I do not regard them as furnishing sound opinion as regards either foreign or domestic policies." There was absolutely nothing to be said, he continued, for "government by a plutocracy, for government by men very powerful in certain lines and gifted with 'the money touch,' but with ideals which in their essence are merely those of so many glorified pawnbrokers." He stood equally, he declared, against government by a plutocracy and government by a mob.

He was fortified by the conviction that he was restoring an older tradition of national purpose—the tradition of the Federalists, about which he had written with such ardor as a young historian. His admiration for Hamilton's conception of government was qualified only by regret over Hamilton's skepticism toward democracy. Jefferson, even though he was right about the plain people, was hopelessly wrong about the role of the state. As Roosevelt's younger friend Henry L. Stimson liked to put it, government was not "a mere organized police force, a sort of necessary evil, but rather an affirmative agency of national progress and social betterment."

For national government to do its job, it had to be stronger than any private group in society. Instead of regarding the state as a possible tyrant, "as Jefferson did," said Stimson, "we now look to executive action to protect the individual citizen against the oppression of this unofficial power of business." From very nearly the start of his presidency, Roosevelt was engaged in battles to vindicate the national will against its boldest domestic challengers—the trusts and combines, the court favorites of earlier Republican rule.

Roosevelt's warfare against the trusts was neither very consistent nor very effective. But his uncertainty derived less from political expediency than from the fact that he had a more complex vision of the problem than the old-fashioned trust busters. For a man like La Follette, with his ruthless simplicities, the Sherman Antitrust Act remained "the strongest, most perfect weapon which the ingenuity of man could forge for the protection of the people against the power and sordid greed of monopoly." But for Roosevelt, who discerned an evolutionary necessity in economic concentration, the Sherman Act was an exercise in nostalgia.

Herbert Croly's *The Promises of American Life,* published in 1909, the year when Roosevelt left the Presidency, added little to Roosevelt's program. But it gave his instinct for national assertion a persuasive setting in political philosophy. In a thoughtful reconsideration of the national experience, Croly saw the essence of the American faith in the careless belief that the nation was "predestined to success by its own adequacy." The promise of American life had been too long considered somehow self-fulfilling; the same automatic processes which had taken care of the past would take care of the future. Croly sharply challenged this whole spirit of optimism and drift. The traditional American confidence in individual freedom, he said, had resulted in a morally and socially undesirable distribution of wealth under which "the ideal Promise, instead of being automatically fulfilled, may well be automatically stifled." The only hope was to transform the national attitude toward social development, to convert the old unconscious sense of national destiny into a conscious sense of national purpose, to replace drift by management. What this meant, Croly said, was that the national state would have to take an active and detailed responsibility for economic and social conditions. It meant a "more highly socialized democracy," a "new nationalism." The theory of the Sherman Act, he added, operated as a "fatal bar" to national planning.

Croly was more interested in affirming a viewpoint than in designing a program; but others were ready to give the New Nationalism its economics. George W. Perkins of J. P. Morgan and Company, himself one of the great trust organizers, felt that modern technology had revolutionized the world and ren-

dered old-style competition obsolete. "What underlies ruthless competitive methods?" Perkins asked. "The desire to supply the public with better goods at a lower price? Is that the moving, impelling force behind it? Nonsense!" Competition, he said, was simply a struggle for power at the expense of everything else. "The entire path of our industrial progress is strewn with the white bones of just such competition." What had given us exploitation, evil working conditions, unemployment, low wages? Competition! "The Congressman who stands for a literal enforcement of the Sherman Act," declared Perkins, "stands for the sweat shop and child labor." Competition had become "too destructive to be tolerated. Co-operation must be the order of the day."

The national government, Perkins said, had first undertaken the supervision of the states, then of the banks, then of the railroad; now, he said, it must undertake the supervision of big business. Let the government license all interstate corporations; and let the licensing system enforce federal standards with respect to capitalization, trade practices, prices, and labor policy. As for corporations, they must recognize that they had obligations to labor and to the public as well as to their stockholders. Let them work out plans for co-partnership; let them, as he put it in a clumsy but expressive phrase, "people-ize" modern industry; let them devise plans for profit-sharing, for social insurance, for old-age pensions. In true co-partnership, said Perkins, there would be "socialism of the highest, best and most ideal sort"—socialism, in other words, which preserved the right of private property.

Perkins was sincerely impressed by the advantages of the German cartel system

—for social security, for economic stability, for industrial growth, for national unity—and he wanted to propel American economic development in the same direction. In 1910 he left Morgan's and went up and down the country, preaching the gospel to any group that would listen. In 1912 he gave over $250,000 to Roosevelt's campaign. As for T.R., he valued Perkins's ideas as much as his money.

T.R. discovered further stimulus in a book published in the spring of 1912—*Concentration and Control: A Solution of the Trust Problem in the United States,* written by Charles R. Van Hise, a classmate of La Follette's at the University of Wisconsin and later the university's president. Agreeing with Perkins about the inevitability of concentration, Van Hise asserted even more strongly the indispensability of control. "If we allow concentration and co-operation," he wrote, "there must be control in order to protect the people, and adequate control is only possible through the administrative commission."

As his own thought clarified, and as his resentment of William Howard Taft, his successor in the Presidency, grew, Roosevelt became increasingly specific. Trust busting seemed to him madness— "futile madness." "It is preposterous to abandon all that has been wrought in the application of the cooperative idea in business and to return to the era of cutthroat competition." But acceptance of bigness could not be allowed to mean surrender to bigness: this was the test of democratic government. "The man who wrongly holds that every human right is secondary to his profit," Roosevelt declared, "must now give way to the advocate of human welfare, who rightly maintains that every man holds his property subject to the general right of the community to regulate its use to whatever degree the public welfare may require it." *To whatever degree:* this was strong language, even for Teddy Roosevelt.

One other force contributed vitally to Roosevelt's developing philosophy. Mastery of private bigness was only half the job; the other half was help for the individual cast adrift in the great society. Here the New Nationalism absorbed the new experience of social work as well as the new teachings of the Social Gospel.

Both the Social Gospel and social work had arisen in the late nineteenth century as nonpolitical responses to the miseries and injustices of the industrial order. Socially-minded ministers began to remind their parishioners that Christians had duties toward their fellow men, that Christian morality was relevant to slums and sweatshops, and that the Christian task would not be completed until the social order itself had been Christianized. "The Christian law," said Dr. Washington Gladden, "is meant to live by, to do business by, to rule politics." When society was transformed by Christian faith, "rotten politics and grinding monopolies would shrivel and disappear; under its banner light and beauty, peace and plenty, joy and gladness would be led in."

This goal, the advocates of the Social Gospel reckoned, could be achieved within history; the Kingdom of God would, in due time, realize itself on earth. But it could not be achieved by the churches alone. "There is a certain important work to be done," wrote Gladden, "which no voluntary organization can succeed in doing—a work which requires the exercise of the power of the state." Nor was this likely to be the existing state, controlled as it was by the business class. "If the banner of the Kingdom of God is to enter through the gates of the future," said Walter Rauschenbusch, the most searching theologian of the Social Gospel, "it will have to be carried by the tramping hosts of labor."

Gladden and Rauschenbusch, in rousing the conscience of modern Protestantism, thus predisposed it both toward an affirmative theory of the state and toward a belief that the power of business must be offset by the power of labor. The formation of such organizations as the Methodist Federation for Social Service in 1907 and the Federal Council of Churches in 1908 signaled the spread of the Social Gospel through the Protestant churches.

What was faith for the apostles of the Social Gospel became works for the men and women of the settlement houses. The first heroine of social work was Jane Addams of Hull-House on Halsted Street in Chicago. Soon after, Lillian Wald set up the Henry Street Settlement in New York. Hull-House, Henry Street, and their counterparts in other cities gave the middle class its first extended contact with the life of the working class—with the sweatshops, the child labor, the unsanitary working conditions, the long hours, the starvation wages, the denial of the right to organize. Relinquishing comfortable middle-class homes, the social workers moved to the city slums and labored to create a breathing-space of hope for the poor, the immigrant, and, above all, for the slum-born children.

This middle-class mission to the poor coincided with the release of energy which came from the new emancipation of women. Hull-House and Henry Street,

in particular, produced an extraordinary group of women whose vitality and compassion reshaped American liberalism. From Hull-House came Florence Kelley, who became the driving force in the National Consumers' League. The idea of the United States Children's Bureau was Lillian Wald's, and its first two chiefs —Julia Lathrop and Grace Abbott—were from Hull-House. The same hopes and ideals fired many younger women—Josephine Goldmark, Frances Perkins, Mary Dewson, Mary Anderson, Edith Abbott. These were the "dedicated old maids." Social work not only relieved their middle-class conscience. It also provided an outlet for their energy in a field which women could make their own.

More than anyone else, Florence Kelley devised the new techniques of social reform. The daughter of W. D. ("Pig-Iron") Kelley, the protectionist congressman, she was a socialist, a friend of Friedrich Engels, and a whirlwind of courage, vigor, and, in Frances Perkins's phrase, "blazing moral indignation." The National Consumers' League had been established in 1899 on the belief that the customer who bought sweatshop goods was as much the employer of sweated labor as the boss of the shop. Under Florence Kelley's direction, the League battled against home manufacturers in tenements, against child labor, against night work and excessive hours for women. The League's investigations turned up facts to stir the public conscience. Then the League's lawyers drafted bills, and the League's lobbyists sought to push them through legislatures. The League thus initiated the fight for minimum-wage laws and worked out a model statute, soon enacted in thirteen states and the District of Columbia. When the law was challenged in the courts, Florence Kelley rushed up to Boston to ask Louis D. Brandeis to argue its constitutionality. For this purpose Brandeis invented the famous "Brandeis brief," which introduced the heresy that the facts as well as the law were relevant to determinations of community health and welfare.

Organizations like the Women's Trade Union League and the Association for Labor Legislation carried on other aspects of the fight for decent labor standards. It was from these middle-class groups, and not from the trade unions, that the first demand came for the abolition of child labor, for maximum-hour and minimum-wage laws, and for social insurance. And the opposition these reformers met from many businessmen—an opposition often camouflaged as solicitude for the "freedom" of women to work twelve hours a day or of seven-year-old children to strip tobacco leaves or twist artificial flowers in slum tenements—deepened suspicion of business motives.

Hull-House, Henry Street, the Consumers' League, and the other organizations educated a whole generation in social responsibility. Henry Morgenthau, Jr., Herbert Lehman, and Adolf A. Berle, Jr., all worked at Henry Street; Frances Perkins, Gerard Swope, and Charles A. Beard at Hull-House (where John Dewey was an early member of the board of trustees); Sidney Hillman at both Hull-House and Henry Street; Joseph B. Eastman at Robert A. Woods's South End House in Boston; an Iowa boy coming east from Grinnell College in 1912 went to work at Christadora House on the lower East Side of New York; his name, Harry Hopkins. Through Belle Moskowitz the social work ethos infected Alfred E. Smith; through Frances Perkins and others, Robert F. Wagner; through Eleanor Roosevelt, active in the Women's Trade Union League and a friend of Florence Kelley's and Lillian Wald's, Franklin D. Roosevelt.

And, for all the appearance of innocence and defenselessness the social workers' apparatus wielded power. "One could not overestimate," observed Wagner, "the central part played by social workers in bringing before their representatives in Congress and state legislatures the present and insistent problems of modern-day life." The subtle and persistent saintliness of the social workers was in the end more deadly than all the bluster of business. Theirs was the implacability of gentleness.

Among politicians, no one responded more alertly than Theodore Roosevelt. In the early eighties he had led the fight in the New York legislature against cigarmaking in tenement houses. As President, he hailed the Consumers' League as early as 1907; and his White House conference on children gave social work, said Jane Addams, "a dignity and a place in the national life which it never had before." Nor was the alliance unnatural. The inner logic of social work was, to a considerable degree, *noblesse oblige* and paternalistic; the bias was more toward helping people than toward enabling them to help themselves. The caseworker often felt she knew best. T.R. always knew best too.

In the meantime, the Progressives in the Republican party were pressing their battle against the Taft administration. La Follette had been their original candidate; but early in 1912 Roosevelt announced his availability. When the Republican convention renominated Taft, Roosevelt decided to quit the party. Before his own convention, he met with a group of leading social workers and adopted a program recently drawn up by the National Conference of Social Work. "Our best plank," he later wrote of the Progressive platform, "the plank which has really given our party its distinctive character, came from them. . . . [The social workers] are doing literally invaluable work." At the convention, Jane Addams was among those seconding his nomination.

Roosevelt's movement reached its climax at Chicago in August. Before a crowd gone mad, T.R., strong as a bull moose, challenged his followers to stand at Armageddon and battle for the Lord. Across the nation young men rose to his call: Gifford Pinchot of Pennsylvania; Harold Ickes and Donald Richberg of Illinois; William Allen White and Alfred M. Landon of Kansas; George W. Norris of Nebraska; Frank Knox of Michigan; Henry A. Wallace of Iowa; Felix Frankfurter and Norman Thomas of New York; Francis Biddle of Pennsylvania; John G. Winant and Charles W. Tobey of New Hampshire; Dean Acheson of Connecticut.

The New Freedom

For their part, the Democrats in 1912 nominated Woodrow Wilson, the governor of New Jersey. Wilson brought qualities as unusual as those of Theodore Roosevelt to American politics. The two men had much in common: cultivation, knowledge, literary skill, personal magnetism, relentless drive. But, where Roosevelt was unbuttoned and expansive, Wilson was reserved and cool; no one known to history ever called him "Woody" or "W.W." Both were lay preachers, but where Roosevelt was a revivalist, bullying his listeners to hit the sawdust trail, Wilson had the severe eloquence of a Calvinist divine. Roose-

velt's egotism overflowed his personality; Wilson's was a hard concentrate within. Roosevelt's power lay in what he did, Wilson's in what he held in reserve.

Erect in bearing, quick in movement, tidy in dress, with sharp eyes and a belligerent jaw, Wilson, when not overcome by self-righteousness or moral fervor, had humor and charm. For all his professorial background, he showed considerable aptitude for politics. He was, in particular, a powerful orator—as the nation discovered in 1912 when he outlined his alternative to the New Nationalism in a series of notable speeches. Declaring "a new social age, a new era of human relationships . . . a new economic society," Wilson summoned his countrymen to the task of liberating the nation from the new tyranny of concentrated wealth. "When we undertake the strategy which is going to be necessary to overcome and destroy this far-reaching system of monopoly," he said, "we are rescuing the business of this country, we are not injuring it; and when we separate the interests from each other and dismember these communities of connection, we have in mind . . . that vision which sees that no society is renewed from the top but that every society is renewed from the bottom." This was the New Freedom.

Wilson vigorously rejected theories of the paternal state. Hamilton had no charm for him: "a great man, but, in my judgment, not a great American." The philosophy of America was equal rights for all and special privileges for none—"a free field and no favor." "I do not want to live under a philanthropy," Wilson said. "I do not want to be taken care of by the government. . . . We do not want a benevolent government. We want a free and a just government."

He cherished the Jeffersonian dream.

Yet he began to give his Jeffersonianism significant new inflections. As he had read the "spirit of Jefferson" as late as 1906, it had enjoined him to eschew nearly all forms of public intervention in the economy. But the very goal of dismantling the system of special privilege called for action by the state. In the end, he set the Jeffersonian theory of the state on its head: "I feel confident that if Jefferson were living in our day he would see what we see. . . . Without the watchful interference, the resolute interference of the government, there can be no fair play." And his experience as governor soon increased his tolerance of governmental power. Political ambition at the same time sharpened his sensitivity to popular discontents; and contacts with William G. McAdoo and Louis D. Brandeis in the 1912 campaign completed the transformation of his Jeffersonianism from a counsel of inaction to a doctrine with a cutting edge. Under the pressure of responsibility, he was coming to see that if he aspired to Jeffersonian ends he might have to relinquish Jeffersonian means.

In McAdoo, Wilson found a businessman with a free-wheeling operator's animus toward Wall Street and with developed ideas about business reform. A Georgian by birth, a New Yorker by residence, a lawyer by training, a promoter by temperament, McAdoo, who was forty-nine years old in 1912, had built the first tunnel under the Hudson and was now president of the Hudson and Manhattan Railroad Company. Tough and energetic, he observed insistently to the business community that corporations must be the servants, not the masters, of the people; that "the public be damned" approach had to be replaced by "the public be pleased." His reading of America's economic development was diametrically opposite to that of George W. Perkins. Where Perkins wrote that the modern corporation's underlying cause was "not the greed of man for wealth and power, but the working of natural causes—of evolution," McAdoo rejoined, "These great combinations are not the *natural* outgrowth of new economic conditions and complex civilization. They are more likely the artificial product of the unrestrained activities of ambitious men of highly-developed acquisitive power."

What could be done about them? "For my part," replied McAdoo, "I believe that all the powers of the nation should be exerted to preserve competitive conditions." Regulation could be attempted; but regulation was only possible through commissions; and the real question was, Who would control the commissons? "Unregulated competition is better than regulated monopoly," said McAdoo early in 1911, thrusting some new phrases into the controversy, "but regulated competition is better than either."

Louis D. Brandeis carried the analysis a few steps farther. Born in 1856 in Louisville, Kentucky, Brandeis had graduated from the Harvard Law School and then settled down to an immensely successful law practice in Boston. His analytical brilliance and his tenacious advocacy won him the clients who could pay most for these talents. By 1907 Brandeis was a millionaire. But, for an idealist, bred in the tradition of the Revolution of 1848, material success was hardly enough. Beginning in the nineties, he had developed a second career— this time as a "people's lawyer," working without fee in the public interest, moving from local problems (streetcar franchises) to state (savings bank life insurance) and then to regional (the

New Haven railroad). Starting in 1907, he came to national attention as counsel for the Consumers' League in a series of notable tests of hours and wages legislation.

He was a tall, stooped figure, with longish gray hair, deep-set eyes, a face of melacholy nobility and brooding wisdom, and something of the aspect of a Jewish Lincoln. In combat, his wrath aroused, he displayed the stern righteousness of an Old Testament prophet; this sometimes made it hard for him to believe that his opponents, too, had honest motives. But, in relaxation, talking among friends, a tinge of Kentucky drawl still in his voice, he had rare serenity of spirit.

For Wilson, Jeffersonianism had been a faith; Brandeis seemed to transform it into a policy. He bluntly denied the major premise of the New Nationalists. Economic bigness, he said, was not inevitable. It did not come from the necessities of the machine age. It was not the inescapable result of the movement toward efficiency. It was the creation, not of technology, but of finance. It sprang from the manipulations of the bankers, eager to float new securities and water new stocks.

The mania for consolidation, Brandeis believed, could end only in the strangling of freedom: J. P. Morgan was the socialists' best friend, because, after he was through with his work, socialism would have so little left to do. "Just as Emperor Nero is said to have remarked in regard to his people that he wished that the Christians had but one neck that he might cut it off by a single blow of his sword, so they say here: 'Let these men gather these things together; they will soon have them all under one head, and by a single act we will take over the whole industry.'"

Where Croly was concerned with the morale of the nation, Brandeis was concerned with the morality of the individual. The curse was bigness: "we are now coming to see that big things may be very bad and mean." For, though business and government might increase indefinitely, men would always remain the same size. Excessive power was the great corrupter. To bestow more power on men than they could endure was to change the few into tyrants, while it destroyed the rest. Centralization enfeebled society by choking off experiment and draining talent from the community into the center. Nor could one pin faith on government regulation: "remedial institutions are apt to fall under the control of the enemy and to become instruments of oppression." In the end responsibility was the only developer— the institutions of the state and the economy must be proportioned to the capabilities of man. The growth of the individual, Brandeis concluded, was "both a necessary means and the end sought."

Here was the reformulation of Jeffersonianism toward which Wilson had been groping. His first meeting with Brandeis in August 1912 was an instant success. The problem, Wilson agreed, was not to regulate monopoly but to regulate competition; and he soon asked Brandeis for a program. Competition, Brandeis replied, could and should be maintained in every branch of private industry. Where monopoly could not be avoided, industry should be "owned by the people and not by the capitalists." Government regulation of monopoly, he continued, was a delusion; either break the power up or take it over. The nation must choose between industrial absolutism, tempered by government control, and industrial liberty.

Thus the New Freedom, and to this

summons, too, young men rallied—W. G. McAdoo and Franklin Delano Roosevelt of New York, Cordell Hull of Tennessee, John N. Garner and Sam Rayburn of Texas, Homer Cummings of Connecticut, Dan Roper of North Carolina, Joseph E. Davies of Wisconsin.

Nationalizing the New Freedom

The partisans of 1912 had no doubt that they were debating fundamentals. To the followers of Wilson, the New Nationalism was a menacing tyranny, in which the twin giants of business and government would grind the individual to sand. To the followers of Roosevelt, the New Freedom harked back impotently to the Jeffersonian past—Jeffersonianism restated, to be sure, in terms of finance capitalism, but obsolete nonetheless in the assumption that the system, once reformed, could run by itself. Wilson and Roosevelt thus raged at each other over the trust issue as if they stood on opposite sides of an impassable abyss. "This difference in the economic policy of the two parties," declared Brandeis in 1912, "is fundamental and irreconcilable." The New Nationalists could not agree more. Nor did Wilson's election and his initial policies reassure them. As late as 1914 Croly dismissed Wilson's program as a mere "revival of Jeffersonian individualism," lacking in a sense of national purpose, oblivious to the fact that "the nationalism of Hamilton, with all its aristocratic leaning, was more democratic, because more constructively social, than the indiscriminate individualism of Jefferson." The young historian Charles A. Beard, fresh from his bold researches into the origins of the Constitution, concurred: agrarian democracy had been Jefferson's futile ambition, "just as the equally unreal and unattainable democracy of small business is Wilson's goal."

The acute and fluent journalist Walter Lippmann, only lately resigned from the Socialist party, contrasted the Wilsonian policy of drift with the Rooseveltian policy of mastery. As George Perkins summed it up with scorn, the "New Freedom had better be called the Old Bondage."

But the gap soon turned out to be less impassable than it had first appeared. Roosevelt did not—as Wilson charged—want to make monopoly universal, any more than Wilson—as Roosevelt replied—wanted to break up every corporation in the country. In abusing each other and misrepresenting each other's views, they obscured the fact that their agreements were actually greater than their differences. Whether the objective was to regulate monopoly or competition, the method was to meet the power of business by expanding the power of government. The New Nationalism and the New Freedom alike affirmed the necessity of active intervention in economic life by the state.

Wilson had already accepted this as the logic of twentieth-century Jeffersonianism when he had shifted from his do-nothing position of 1906 to his activism of 1912. "The program of a government of freedom," he said, "must in these days be positive." Even Brandeis, for all his fear of bigness, wanted the state not only to break up the trusts but to carry out an extensive program on behalf of labor and social security.

Others of Wilson's associates looked even more genially on the state. Colonel E. M. House, the quiet and self-effacing Texan, soon to become the new President's confidential adviser, had published in 1912 *Philip Dru, Administrator*, a utopian fantasy in which the hero, fearful in the year 1920 that organized wealth was about to end American freedom, seized power and proclaimed himself dictator. Dru had to divest himself, House noted, of early states-rights predispositions; but he quickly established a strong central regime, put corporations under stringent national control (while declining to limit their size), abolished holding companies, socialized the telephone and telegraph, enacted full employment legislation, decreed federal old-age and unemployment insurance, and in general set up a nationalism so comprehensive that it might even have given Theodore Roosevelt pause. Yet, by 1918, Franklin K. Lane, Wilson's Secretary of the Interior noted, "All that book has said should be, comes about slowly, even woman suffrage. The President comes to *Philip Dru* in the end."

Still, it was less advice than circumstance which caused Wilson to begin to bridge the abyss. The first pressure came from the radical wing of the southern Democrats. Southerners of a more genteel stripe, like Carter Glass of Virginia and Oscar W. Underwood of Alabama, were well satisfied with the New Freedom of 1912. But some of their colleagues had a more active conception of government. Congressman Cordell Hull wanted a federal income tax. Congressman Sam Rayburn, with Brandeis's assistance, had drawn up a bill to control the marketing of railroad securities. And, for the agrarian Democrats of the Bryan school, champions of the cracker and the redneck, haters of Wall Street, the first New Freedom seemed especially meager. It was not enough they felt, to whittle down class legislation for the business community. The Wilson Administration, they believed, had a positive obligation to the poor. It must balance Republican favoritism for big business by doing

something itself for small business and the farmers. The southern radicals had their first triumph when they helped Bryan, Brandeis, and McAdoo force a basic revision of Carter Glass's bill for a Federal Reserve system. Then they made another breach in the conservative conception of the New Freedom by tacking on to the Federal Reserve bill provisions for short-term credits for farmers. Wilson soon found himself accepting what was, by his theory of 1912, class legislation.

At the same time, Wilson began to move in strange new directions in the critical field of antitrust policy. Brandeis, who in 1912 had felt regulation to be worse than useless, now took up the New Nationalist idea of a federal commission to supervise corporations. As a result came the laws of 1914 establishing the Federal Trade Commission and giving it regulatory powers. Worse, Brandeis soon recommended for appointment as chairman of the Commission on Industrial Relations the same Charles Van Hise whose *Concentration and Control* had been T.R.'s bible two years earlier. The "fundamental and irreconcilable" differences of 1912 had lost their sting by 1914.

As the election of 1916 approached, Wilson completed his acceptance of the main lines of the Progressive program of 1912. He now stood clearly for strong government, for administrative regulation, for some intervention on behalf of the farmer and the worker—in short, for affirmative federal action aimed to produce equality of opportunity. In a basic respect, Roosevelt seemed to have been right: the people's government had to be stronger than business if popular rule were to be effective.

RICHARD HOFSTADTER (1916–   ), DeWitt
Clinton Professor of American History at Columbia
University since 1959, has been as influential a critic
as Arthur Schlesinger has been a partisan of the liberal
tradition. Neither Progressivism nor the New Deal, he
writes below, went far enough toward a philosophy
of central planning. Does the evidence support him
against Schlesinger that the Wilson administration did
not enact the substance of the New Nationalism?
Not only evidence, but one's values as well, are
involved in assessing Hofstadter's moral judgment
that the Progressives, epitomized by Wilson, were
backward in wanting to restore the avarice of
economic individualism.*

Woodrow Wilson: Democrat in Cupidity

The most common vision of national
life, in its fondness for the panoramic
backward gaze, has been that of the
observation-car platform.

Although the national nostalgia has
intensified in the last decade, it is by no
means new. It has a history of its own,
particularly in political traditions. A
longing to recapture the past, in fact, has
itself been such a basic ingredient of the
recent American past that no history of
political thinking is complete which does
not attempt to explain it. In American
politics the development of a retro-
spective and nostalgic cast of mind has
gone hand in hand with the slow decline

of a traditional faith. When competition
and enterprise were rising, men thought
of the future; when they were flourishing, of the present. Now—in an age of
concentration, bigness, and corporate
monopoly—when competition and opportunity have gone into decline, men
look wistfully back toward a golden age.

In the early days of the Republic the
Founding Fathers, despite their keen
sense of history, felt that they were
founding novel institutions and gloried
in the newness of what they were doing.
As the decades passed, this feeling faded.
Where the Founding Fathers dreamed of
and planned for a long-term future, the

* Reprinted from *The American Political Tradition and the Men Who Made It* by
Richard Hofstadter, by permission of Alfred A. Knopf, Inc. Copyright 1948 by Alfred A.
Knopf, Inc.

generation of Webster, Clay, and Calhoun was busily absorbed with a profitable present. The following generation, North and South, was consciously concerned to preserve and defend what its fathers had built. Lincoln, for example, believed that he was stabilizing his America and erecting bulwarks against undesirable change. Although he helped to form a new party, uprooted slavery and the aristocracy of the South, led a revolutionary change in the structure of national power, and paved the way for the success of industrial capitalism, he did all these things with the intent of restoring the Union as it had been, saving the common man's control of the government, and protecting the existing rights of free labor.

The post Civil War generation, witnessing a spurt of economic expansion, lived once again in the present and the future. But beginning with the time of Bryan, the dominant American ideal has been steadily fixed on bygone institutions and conditions. In early twentieth-century progressivism this backward-looking vision reached the dimensions of a major paradox. Such heroes of the progressive revival as Bryan, La Follette, and Wilson proclaimed that they were trying to undo the mischief of the past forty years and re-create the old nation of limited and decentralized power, genuine competition, democratic opportunity, and enterprise. As Wilson put it, the machinery of democratic government was to be revivified *"for the purpose of recovering what seems to have been lost . . . our old variety and freedom and individual energy of development."* Even Theodore Roosevelt, who realized and at times candidly stated the impossibility of any such undertaking, so far as it concerned the country's economic structure, was careful to do things that caused

him to be acclaimed as a "trust-buster."

Among postwar statesmen, Herbert Hoover, who is not usually thought to have much in common with these men of the progressive era—and whose methods and temper, in fact, were quite different—still adhered to much the same premises and accepted the same goals. Like the progressives, he expected to see a brilliant and expansive future, but he expected to reach it along the traditional highway. Franklin D. Roosevelt stands out among the statesmen of modern American liberalism—and indeed among all statesmen since Hamilton—for his sense of the failure of tradition, his recognition of the need for novelty and daring. His capacity for innovation in practical measures was striking, and the New Deal marked many deviations in the American course; but his capacity for innovation in ideas was far from comparable; he was neither systematic nor consistent, and he provided no clearly articulated break with the inherited faith. Although it has been said repeatedly that we need a new conception of the world to replace the ideology of self-help, free enterprise, competition, and beneficent cupidity upon which Americans have been nourished since the foundation of the Republic, no new conceptions of comparable strength have taken root and no statesman with a great mass following has arisen to propound them. Bereft of a coherent and plausible body of belief—for the New Deal, if it did little more, went far to undermine old ways of thought—Americans have become more receptive than ever to dynamic personal leadership as a substitute. This is part of the secret of Roosevelt's popularity, and, since his death, of the rudderless and demoralized state of American liberalism.

The following studies in the ideology of American statesmanship have convinced me of the need for a reinterpretation of our political traditions which emphasizes the common climate of American opinion. The existence of such a climate of opinion has been much obscured by the tendency to place political conflict in the foreground of history. It is generally recognized that American politics has involved, among other things, a series of conflicts between special interests—between landed capital and financial or industrial capital, between old and new enterprises, large and small property—and that it has not shown, at least until recently, many signs of a struggle between the propertied and unpropertied classes. What has not been sufficiently recognized is the consequence for political thought. The fierceness of the political struggles has often been misleading; for the range of vision embraced by the primary contestants in the major parties has always been bounded by the horizons of property and enterprise. However much at odds on specific issues, the major political traditions have shared a belief in the rights of property, the philosophy of economic individualism, the value of competition; they have accepted the economic virtues of capitalist culture as necessary qualities of man. Even when some property right has been challenged—as it was by followers of Jefferson and Jackson—in the name of the rights of man or the rights of the community, the challenge, when translated into practical policy, has actually been urged on behalf of some other kind of property.

The sanctity of private property, the right of the individual to dispose of and invest it, the value of opportunity, and the natural evolution of self-interest and self-assertion, within broad legal limits, into a beneficent social order have been staple tenets of the central faith in American political ideologies; these conceptions have been shared in large part by men as diverse as Jefferson, Jackson, Lincoln, Cleveland, Bryan, Wilson, and Hoover. The business of politics—so the creed runs—is to protect this competitive world, to foster it on occasion, to patch up its incidental abuses, but not to cripple it with a plan for common collective action. American traditions also show a strong bias in favor of equalitarian democracy, but it has been a democracy in cupidity rather than a democracy of fraternity.

Almost the entire span of American history under the present Constitution has coincided with the rise and spread of modern industrial capitalism. In material power and productivity the United States has been a flourishing success. Societies that are in such good working order have a kind of mute organic consistency. They do not foster ideas that are hostile to their fundamental working arrangements. Such ideas may appear, but they are slowly and persistently insulated, as an oyster deposits nacre around an irritant. They are confined to small groups of dissenters and alienated intellectuals, and except in revolutionary times they do not circulate among practical politicians. The range of ideas, therefore, which practical politicians can conveniently believe in is normally limited by the climate of opinion that sustains their culture. They differ, sometimes bitterly, over current issues, but they also share a general framework of ideas which makes it possible for them to co-operate when the campaigns are over.

... It is in the nature of politics that conflict stands in the foreground, and historians usually abet the politicians in keeping it there. Two special interests, striving to gain control of government policy, will invoke somewhat different ideas to promote their causes. The material interests in good time will be replaced by others as the economic order changes, but their ideas, which already have wide acceptance, will be adapted again and again with slight changes to new conditions. Later generations, finding certain broad resemblances between their own problems and those of an earlier age, will implicitly take sides with the campaigners of former years; historians, who can hardly be quite free of partisanship, reconstruct the original conflict from the surviving ideas that seem most intelligible in the light of current experience and current conviction. Hence the issues of the twentieth century are still debated in the language of Jefferson's time, and our histories of the Jefferson era are likewise influenced by twentieth-century preconceptions that both Jefferson and his opponents might have found strange. While the conflicts of Jefferson's day are constantly reactivated and thus constantly brought to mind, the commonly shared convictions are neglected.

These shared convictions are far from unimportant. Although the Jeffersonians and Federalists raged at each other with every appearance of a bitter and indissoluble opposition, differences in practical policy boiled down to a very modest minimum when Jefferson took power, and before long the two parties were indistinguishable. If their ideas are to be tested in action, we must give due weight to the relatively slight differences in policies that they gave rise to. This seems to me to be one of the keys to historical analysis because it leads us to consider the common end at which, willy-nilly, both Jefferson and the Federalists arrived. The same principle can profitably be extended to the rest of American history. And if it is true of

some of the more serious conflicts, how much more true will it be of the innumerable presidential campaigns in which the area of agreement was so large and the area of disagreement so small that significant issues could never be found! Above and beyond temporary and local conflicts there has been a common ground, a unity of cultural and political tradition, upon which American civilization has stood. That culture has been intensely nationalistic and for the most part isolationist; it has been fiercely individualistic and capitalistic. In a corporate and consolidated society demanding international responsibility, cohesion, centralization, and planning, the traditional ground is shifting under our feet. It is imperative in a time of cultural crisis to gain fresh perspectives on the past. . . .

In the campaign of 1912 Wilson emerged as the middle-of-the-road candidate, flanked on the right by Taft and on the left by Roosevelt in his new pose. The bulk of left-wing reform sentiment went with the Progressive Party, and many moderate Republicans seem to have deserted Taft for Wilson. Since Taft was obviously out of the running, Wilson centered his fire on Theodore Roosevelt and stressed the one issue that chiefly distinguished their points of view—the trusts. Wilson's program, the result of his first serious thinking on the trust problem, was taken from the preachings of Louis D. Brandeis and formulated with the lawyer's guidance. Wilson's speeches, the best parts of which are printed in *The New Freedom,* sound like the collective wail of the American middle class.

What has happened in America, Wilson told the voters, is that industry has ceased to be free because the laws do not prevent the strong from crushing the weak. The best, the most gifted part of the nation, the rising workingman and the thrifty ambitious bourgeois, are being cramped and confined. "The middle class is being more and more squeezed out by the processes which we have been taught to call processes of prosperity." The established interests make a concerted effort to squeeze out the beginner; they cripple his credit; they undersell him in his local market until his business withers on the vine; they discriminate against the retailer who buys from their rival; they withhold raw materials from the small man. In short, they compete unfairly.

Those who criticize the competitive order assert that free competition itself has made it possible for the big to crush the little. This Wilson denied. "I reply, it is not free competition that has done that; it is illicit competition." A big business that survives competition through intelligence, efficiency, and economies deserves to survive. But the trust is "an arrangement to get rid of competition"; it "buys efficiency out of business." "I am for big business," said Wilson, succumbing to the equivocation that invariably creeps into politicians' discussions of the trust problem, "and I am against the trusts." [3]

The interests that have squeezed out the middle class are the same that control politics, Wilson went on. "The government of the United States at present is a foster-child of the special interests." But the people will regain control and return to their old com-petitive, democratic principles. "America will insist upon recovering in practice those ideals which she has always professed." The new order will be woven into the texture of the old: "If I did not believe that to be progressive was to preserve the essentials of our institutions, I for one could not be a progressive."

The New Freedom would address itself to the fundamental problem of the present age. "What this country needs above everything else is a body of laws which will look after the men who are on the make rather than the men who are already made." "The man who is on the make is the judge of what is happening in America, not the man who has made good ... that is the man by whose judgment I, for one, wish to be guided." The hope of the nation, its real creative energies, had always been in the men "out of unknown homes" who rise to be masters of industry and politics.

Wilson conceded that there were many handsome and magnanimous reform proposals in the Progressive platform that stirred all the sympathies of a man of goodwill; but the Progressives were not even proposing to do the fundamental thing, which was to wrestle with the trusts. They proposed instead to work *through* the trusts, to guarantee, as it were, that the trusts would be merciful: "We will make these monopolies kind to you." "But," answered Wilson, "I do not want the sympathy of the trusts for the human race ... their condescending assistance." The procedure Roosevelt stood for led up a blind alley. [4]

---

[3] A position much like that of Albert J. Beveridge at the Progressive Party convention: "We mean to make little business big, and all business honest, instead of striving to make Big Business little, and yet letting it remain dishonest." [Footnotes 1 and 2 occur in the preceding paragraphs that are omitted here—Ed.]

[4] Roosevelt in turn pointed out that New Jersey was one of the most notorious corporation states in the country. After the election Wilson secured the passage of the "Seven Sisters" laws, which placed serious restrictions on corporations within the state. The companies transferred their seat of incorporation to the complaisant neighbor state of Delaware, and New Jersey lost

"You can't find your way to social reform through the forces that have made social reform necessary." The Progressive program was "perfectly agreeable to the monopolies," and for that reason "not a progressive program at all." Its method of pretended trust-control was the method proposed everywhere by "the very men who are interested in the maintenance of the present economic system of the United States."

Shrewdly Wilson exposed the interlocking structure of business and governmental power that would exist under what he called "the Roosevelt plan."

I find, then, the proposition to be this: That there shall be two masters, the great corporation, and over it the government of the United States; and I ask who is going to be master of the government of the United States? It has a master now,—those who in combination control these monopolies. And if the government controlled by the monopolies in its turn controls the monopolies, the partnership is finally consummated.

The conceptions set forth in Wilson's speeches of 1912 were translated into legislation with remarkable success and fidelity during his first four years of office. The first Wilson administration, in fact, produced more positive legislative achievements than any administration since the days of Alexander Hamilton. Professor Lindsay Rogers has observed that the ex-professor "more than any of his predecessors has exerted an almost absolute authority over Congress." Wilson's administration was the first to secure a material downward tariff revision since the Civil War. In the Federal Reserve Act it revamped the nation's banking and credit system and placed it under public control. For the benefit of

the revenue from fees. Later New Jersey again became a notorious home of corporations.

the farmers it passed the Federal Farm Loan Act, putting the government in the business of supplying agricultural credits, and the Warehousing Act, a measure that embodied several provisions of the old Populist independent treasury scheme. Its middle-class program for the control of big business was embodied in the Clayton Act, which was meant to implement the Sherman Anti-Trust Act, and in the creation of the Federal Trade Commission, which was to enjoin what Wilson had called "illicit competition." Labor also won gains, primarily in the clause of the Clayton Act exempting unions from harassment by anti-trust suits, and also in the La Follette Seamen's Act, the Adamson Act (passed under threat of a major railroad strike), setting an eight-hour day for railroad workers in interstate commerce, a child-labor act (soon, however, to be declared unconstitutional in one of the Supreme Court's most curious decisions), and a compensation law for Civil Service workers.[5]

Under a system of finance capitalism the government of the United States can hardly carry on without at least the passive co-operation of the financial community. Within the limits of the possibilities Wilson carried out the work of his first administration in a spirit of independence, a course maintained under the pressure of Bryan's wing of the party and such advisers as Louis D. Brandeis, whose opinions won Wilson's respect.[6] Not warfare, in fact, but simply

[5] The one important Wilson recommendation that was not enacted into law was the proposal that the Interstate Commerce Commission be empowered to regulate the issuance of securities by railroad companies.

[6] A sharp struggle occurred when bankers tried to get control of the proposed Federal Reserve Board. They came to Washington in force, confronted Wilson across his desk, and

a rather uneasy peace was the condition that prevailed between the administration and business up to 1917. Wilson proposed no fundamental alteration in the economic order. He still aimed to preserve competition, individualism, enterprise, opportunity—things that he regarded as vital in the American heritage. He had changed his mind, however, about regulation; his espousal of regulatory legislation by the federal government signified the abandonment of his earlier laissez-faire views. Brandeis had said during the 1912 campaign that the issue was regulated competition versus regulated monopoly, and all but

the die-hards had abandoned the view that the State must keep its hands clear of the economic system. Wilson proposed that the force of the State be used to *restore* pristine American ideals, not to strike out sharply in a new direction. (*"If I did not believe that to be progressive was to preserve the essentials of our institutions, I for one could not be a progressive."*)

After the passage of the Clayton Act and the creation of the Federal Trade Commission, Wilson felt that his basic program had been fulfilled. In his message to Congress, December 8, 1914, he declared:

> Our program of legislation with regard to the regulation of business is now complete. It has been put forth, as we intended as a whole, and leaves no conjecture as to what is to follow. The road at last lies clear and firm before business ... the road to ungrudged, unclouded success.

Essentially the New Freedom was an attempt of the middle class, with agrarian and labor support, to arrest the exploitation of the community, the concentration of wealth, and the growing control of politics by insiders, and to restore, as far as possible, competitive opportunities in business. Walter Lippmann, then in his socialist phase, characterized the New Freedom as "the effort of small business men and farmers to use the government against the larger collective organization of industry." It had no sympathy, he complained, in harsh but essentially accurate language, "for the larger collective life upon which the world is entering." It was "a freedom for the little profiteer, but no freedom from the narrowness, the poor incentives, the limited vision of small competitors . . . from the chaos, the welter, the strategy of industrial war."

---

with a great show of knowledge presented their arguments to the comparative financial innocent in the executive chair. When they had finished, Wilson asked the leaders: "Will one of you gentlemen tell me in what civilized country of the earth there are important government boards of control on which private interests are represented?" After a long silence he inquired: "Which of you gentlemen thinks the railroads should select members of the Interstate Commerce Commission?" These unanswered questions closed discussion of banker control of the Federal Reserve System.

Resentment of Wilson among bankers became intense. Oswald Garrison Villard in his memoirs recalls a luncheon with Thomas W. Lamont of the House of Morgan at which Lamont told him that Wilson had recently refused categorically to receive any member of that firm. Lamont's comment reflects on the curious position of an "independent" administration. What puzzled him, he said, was why the State Department was calling upon the House of Morgan to advance its Central American policies by floating loans. "We are either one thing or the other," he complained. "We are either respectable business men with whom the government can do business or we are not fit to associate with: we can't be both at the same time."

Actually the connection of government and finance continued, although at some remove. As Matthew Josephson emphasizes, the bankers had indirect access to Wilson's mind through his trusted adviser Colonel E. M. House, whom they saw on frequent occasions and who served as a conveyer belt for their views. This process saved Wilson's feeling of independence and integrity, a matter of vital importance to him.

Unlike Hofstadter, who is to the left of the liberal tradition but a liberal reformer all the same, H. L. MENCKEN (1880–1956), the most iconoclastic American journalist of this century, was no reformer at all. The Progressives infuriated him when they did not amuse him. Woodrow Wilson he dismissed as a moralizing fanatic with a second-rate mind, and William Jennings Bryan as an absolute and meddling fool. The Baltimore writer believed not only in a cultivated, disinterested, intelligent elite, but in liberty. He was something of a nineteenth-century liberal. Theodore Roosevelt, attacked below as an American kaiser posing as a liberal, fails most of Mencken's tests for leadership. But note the unexpected conclusion that TR was a "genuine leader" in his "prevision."*

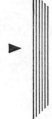

Theodore Roosevelt: Pseudo Liberal

In all this, of course, I strip the process of its plumes and spangles, and expose a chain of causes and effects that Roosevelt himself, if he were alive, would denounce as grossly contumelious to his native purity of spirit—and perhaps in all honesty. It is not necessary to raise any doubts as to that honesty. No one who has given any study to the development and propagation of political doctrine in the United States can have failed to notice how the belief in issues among politicians tends to run in exact ratio to the popularity of those issues. Let the populace begin suddenly to swallow a new panacea or to take fright at a new bugaboo, and almost instantly nine-tenths of the masterminds of politics begin to believe that the panacea is a sure-cure for all the malaises of the Republic, and the bugaboo an immediate and unbearable menace to all law, order and domestic tranquillity.

At the bottom of this singular intellectual resilience, of course, there is a good deal of hard calculation; a man must keep up with the procession of crazes, or his day is swiftly done. But in it there are also considerations a good deal more subtle, and maybe less discreditable. For one thing, a man devoted professionally to patriotism and the wisdom of the fathers is very apt to come to a resigned sort of acquiescence in all

* Reprinted from *A Mencken Chrestomathy* by H. L. Mencken, by permission of Alfred A. Knopf, Inc. Copyright 1920 by Alfred A. Knopf, Inc. Renewed, 1948 by H. L. Mencken.

the doctrinaire rubbish that lies beneath the national scheme of things—to believe, let us say, if not that the plain people are gifted with an infallible sagacity, then at least that they have an inalienable right to see their follies executed. Poll-parroting nonsense as a matter of daily routine, the politician ends by assuming that it is sense, even though he doesn't believe it. For another thing, there is the contagion of mob enthusiasm —a much underestimated murrain. No man is so remote and arctic that he is wholly safe from that contamination; it explains many extravagant phenomena of a democratic society; in particular, it explains why the mob leader is so often a victim to his mob.

Roosevelt, a perfectly typical politician, devoted to the trade, not primarily because he was gnawed by ideals, but because he frankly enjoyed its rough-and-tumble encounters and its gaudy rewards, was probably moved in both ways —and also by the hard calculation that I have mentioned. If, by any ineptness of the British press-agents and tear-squeezers, indignation over the invasion of Belgium had failed to materialize—if, worse still, some gross infringement of American rights by the English had caused it to be forgotten completely—if, finally, Wilson had been whooping for war with the populace firmly against him —in such event it goes without saying that the moral horror of Roosevelt would have stopped short at a very low amperage, and that he would have refrained from making it the center of his polity. But with things as they were, lying neatly to his hand, he permitted it to take on an extraordinary virulence, and before long all his old delight in German militarism had been converted into a lofty detestation of German militarism, and its chief spokesman on this side of the

Atlantic became its chief opponent. Getting rid of that old delight, of course, was not easily achieved. The concrete enthusiasm could be throttled, but the habit of mind remained. Thus one beheld the curious spectacle of militarism belabored in terms of militarism—of the Kaiser arraigned in unmistakably *kaiserliche* tones.

Such violent swallowings and regurgitations were no novelties to the man. His whole political career was marked, in fact, by performances of the same sort. The issues that won him most votes were issues that, at bottom, he didn't believe in; there was always a mental reservation in his rhetoric. He got into politics, not as a tribune of the plain people, but as an amateur reformer of the snobbish type common in the eighties, by the *Nation* out of the Social Register. He was a young Harvard man scandalized by the discovery that his town was run by men with such names as Michael O'Shaunnessy and Terence Googan—that his social inferiors were his political superiors. His sympathies were essentially anti-democratic. He believed in strong centralization—the concentration of power in a few hands, the strict regimentation of the nether herd, the abandonment of platitudes. His heroes were such Federalists as Morris and Hamilton; he made his first splash in the world by writing about them and praising them. Worse, his daily associations were with the old Union League crowd of high-tariff Republicans—men almost apoplectically opposed to every movement from below— safe and sane men, highly conservative and suspicious men—the profiteers of peace, as they afterward became the profiteers of war. His early adventures in politics were not very fortunate, nor did they reveal any capacity for leadership. The bosses of the day took him in rather sportively, played him for what they could get out of him, and then turned him loose. In a few years he became disgusted and went West. Returning after a bit, he encountered catastrophe: as a candidate for Mayor of New York he was drubbed unmercifully. He went back to the West. He was, up to this time, a comic figure—an anti-politician victimized by politicians, a pseudo-aristocrat made ridiculous by the mob-masters he detested.

But meanwhile something was happening that changed the whole color of the political scene, and was destined, eventually, to give Roosevelt his chance. That something was a shifting in what might be called the foundations of reform. Up to now it had been an essentially aristocratic movement—superior, sniffish and anti-democratic. But hereafter it took on a strongly democratic color and began to adopt democratic methods. More, the change gave it new life. What Harvard, the Union League Club and Godkin's *Nation* had failed to accomplish, the plain people now undertook to accomplish. This invasion of the old citadel of virtue was first observed in the West, and its manifestations out there must have given Roosevelt a good deal more disquiet than satisfaction. It is impossible to imagine him finding anything to his taste in the outlandish doings of the Populists, the wild schemes of the pre-Bryan dervishes. His instincts were against all that sort of thing. But as the movement spread toward the East it took on a certain urbanity, and by the time it reached the seaboard it had begun to be almost civilized.

With this new brand of reform Roosevelt now made terms. It was full of principles that outraged all his pruderies, but it at least promised to work. His entire political history thereafter, down

to the day of his death, was a history of compromises with the new forces—of a gradual yielding, for strategic purposes, to ideas that were intrinsically at odds with his congenital prejudices. When, after a generation of that sort of compromising, the so-called Progressive party was organized and he seized the leadership of it from the Westerners who had founded it, he performed a feat of wholesale englutination that must forever hold a high place upon the roll of political prodigies. That is to say, he swallowed at one gigantic gulp, and out of the same herculean jug, the most amazing mixture of social, political and economic sure-cures ever got down by one hero, however valiant, however athirst—a cocktail made up of all the elixirs hawked among the boobery in his time, from woman suffrage to the direct primary, and from the initiative and referendum to the short ballot, and from Prohibition to public ownership, and from trust-busting to the recall of judges.

This homeric achievement made him the head of the most tatterdemalion party even seen in American politics—a party composed of such incompatible ingredients and hung together so loosely that it began to disintegrate the moment it was born. In part it was made up of mere disordered enthusiasts—believers in anything and everything, pathetic victims of the credulity complex, habitual followers of jitney messiahs, incurable hopers and snufflers. But in part it was also made up of rich converts like Roosevelt himself—men eager for office, disappointed by the old parties, and now quite willing to accept any aid that half-idiot doctrinaires could give them. I have no doubt that Roosevelt himself, carried away by the emotional hurricanes of the moment and especially by the quasi-religious monkey-shines that marked the first Progressive convention, gradually convinced himself that at least some of the doctrinaires, in the midst of all their imbecility, yet preached a few ideas that were workable, and perhaps even sound. But at bottom he was against them, and not only in the matter of their specific remedies, but also in the larger matter of their childish faith in the wisdom and virtue of the plain people.

Roosevelt, for all his fluent mastery of democratic counter-words, democratic gestures and all the rest of the armamentarium of the mob-master, had no such faith in his heart of hearts. He didn't believe in democracy; he believed simply in government. His remedy for all the great pangs and longings of existence was not a dispersion of authority, but a hard concentration of authority. He was not in favor of unlimited experiment; he was in favor of a rigid control from above, a despotism of inspired prophets and policemen. He was not for democracy as his followers understood democracy, and as it actually is and must be; he was for a paternalism of the true Bismarckian pattern, almost of the Napoleonic pattern—a paternalism concerning itself with all things, from the regulation of coal-mining and meat-packing to the regulation of spelling and marital rights. His instincts were always those of the property-owning Tory, not those of the romantic Liberal.* Even when, for campaign purposes, he came to terms with the Liberals his thoughts always ranged far afield. When he tackled the trusts the thing that he had in his mind's eye

* In an earlier version of this article Mencken made the point more strongly: "All the fundamental objects of Liberalism—free speech, unhampered enterprise, the least possible governmental interference—were abhorrent to him." *Prejudices: Second Series* (New York, 1920), 124—Ed.

was not the restoration of competition but the subordination of all private trusts to one great national trust, with himself at its head. And when he attacked the courts it was not because they put their own prejudices before the law but because they refused to put *his* prejudices before the law.

In all his career no one ever heard him make an argument for the rights of the citizen; his eloquence was always expended in expounding the duties of the citizen. I have before me a speech in which he pleaded for "a spirit of kindly justice toward every man and woman," but that seems to be as far as he ever got in that direction—and it was the gratuitous justice of the absolute monarch that he apparently had in mind, not the autonomous and inalienable justice of a free society. The duties of the citizen, as he understood them, related not only to acts, but also to thoughts. There was, to his mind, a simple body of primary doctrine, and dissent from it was the foulest of crimes. No man could have been more bitter against opponents, or more unfair to them, or more ungenerous. In this department, indeed, even so gifted a specialist in dishonorable controversy as Wilson seldom surpassed him. He never stood up to a frank and chivalrous debate. He dragged herrings across the trail. He made seductive faces at the gallery. He capitalized his enormous talents as an entertainer, his rank as a national hero, his public influence and consequence. The two great law-suits in which he was engaged were screaming burlesques upon justice. He tried them in the newspapers before ever they were called; he befogged them with irrelevant issues; his appearances in court were not the appearances of a witness standing on a level with other witnesses, but those of a comedian sure of his crowd. He was, in his dealings with concrete men as in his dealings with men in the mass, a charlatan of the very highest skill—and there was in him, it goes without saying, the persuasive charm of the charlatan as well as the daring deviousness, the humanness of naïveté as well as the humanness of chicane. He knew how to woo— and not only boobs.

The appearance of such men, of course, is inevitable under democracy. Consummate showmen, they arrest the wonder of the mob, and so put its suspicions to sleep. What they actually believe is of secondary consequence; the main thing is what they say; even more, the way they say it. Obviously, their activity does a great deal of damage to the democratic theory, for they are standing refutations of the primary doctrine that the common folk choose their leaders wisely. They damage it again in another and more subtle way. That is to say, their ineradicable contempt for the minds they must heat up and bamboozle leads them into a fatalism that shows itself in a cynical and opportunistic politics, a deliberate avoidance of fundamentals. The policy of a democracy thus becomes an eternal improvisation, changing with the private ambitions of its leaders and the transient and often unintelligible emotions of its rank and file. Roosevelt, incurably undemocratic in his habits of mind, often found it difficult to gauge those emotional oscillations. The fact explains his frequent loss of mob support, his periodical journeys into Coventry. There were times when his magnificent talents as a public comedian brought the proletariat to an almost unanimous groveling at his feet, but there were also times when he puzzled and dismayed it, and so awakened its hostility.

I have a notion that he died too soon. His best days were probably not behind him, but ahead of him. Had he lived ten years longer, he might have enjoyed a great rehabilitation, and exchanged his old false leadership of the inflammatory and fickle mob for a sound and true leadership of the civilized minority. For the more one studies his mountebankeries as mob-master, the more one is convinced that there was a shrewd man beneath the motley, and that his actual beliefs were anything but nonsensical. The truth of them, indeed, emerges more clearly day by day. The old theory of a federation of free and autonomous states has broken down by its own weight, and we are moved toward centralization by forces that have long been powerful and are now quite irresistible. So with the old theory of national isolation: it, too, has fallen to pieces. The United States can no longer hope to lead a separate life in the world, undisturbed by the pressure of foreign aspirations. Roosevelt, by whatever route of reflection or intuition, arrived at a sense of these facts at a time when it was still somewhat scandalous to state them, and it was the capital effort of his life to reconcile them, in some dark way or other, to the prevailing platitudes, and so get them heeded. Today no one seriously maintains, as all Americans once maintained, that the States can go on existing together as independent commonwealths, each with its own laws, its own legal theory and its own view of the common constitutional bond. And today no one seriously maintains, as all Americans once maintained, that the nation may safely potter on without adequate means of defense. However unpleasant it may be to contemplate, the fact is plain that the American people, during the next century, will have to fight to maintain their place in the sun.

Roosevelt lived just long enough to see

his notions in these directions take on life, but not long enough to see them openly adopted. To the extent of his prevision he was a genuine leader of the nation, and perhaps in the years to come, when his actual ideas are disentangled from the demogogic fustian in which he had to wrap them, his more honest pronunciamentoes will be given canonical honors, and he will be ranked among the prophets. He saw clearly more than one other thing that was by no means obvious to his age—for example, the inevitability of frequent wars under the new world-system of extreme nationalism; again, the urgent necessity, for primary police ends, of organizing the backward nations into groups of vassals, each under the hoof of some first-rate power; yet again, the probability of the breakdown of the old system of free competition; once more, the high social utility of the Spartan virtues and the grave dangers of sloth and ease; finally, the incompatibility of free speech and democracy. I do not say that he was always quite honest, even when he was most indubitably right. But in so far as it was possible for him to be honest and exist at all politically, he inclined toward the straightforward thought and the candid word. That is to say, his instinct prompted him to tell the truth, just as the instinct of Wilson prompted him to shift and dissimulate. What ailed him was the fact that his lust for glory, when it came to a struggle, was always vastly more powerful than his lust for the eternal verities. Tempted sufficiently, he would sacrifice anything and everything to get applause. Thus the statesman was debauched by the politician, and the philosopher was elbowed out of sight by the popinjay.

What he stood most clearly in opposition to was the superior pessimism of the three Adams brothers—the notion that the public problems of a democracy are unworthy the thought and effort of a civilized and self-respecting man—the same error that lies in wait for all of us who hold ourselves above the general. Against this suicidal aloofness Roosevelt always hurled himself with brave effect. Enormously sensitive and resilient, almost pathological in his appetite for activity, he made it plain to everyone that the most stimulating sort of sport imaginable was to be obtained in fighting, not for mere money, but for ideas. There was no aristocratic reserve about him. He was not, in fact, an aristocrat at all, but a quite typical member of the upper *bourgeoisie*. The marks of the thoroughbred were simply not there. The man was blatant, crude, overly confidential, devious, tyrannical, vainglorious, sometimes quite childish. One often observed in him a certain pathetic wistfulness, a reaching out for a grand manner that was utterly beyond him. But the sweet went with the bitter. He had all the virtues of the fat and complacent burgher. His disdain of affectation and prudery was magnificent. He hated all pretension save his own pretension. He had a sound respect for hard effort, for loyalty, for thrift, for honest achievement.

His worst defects were the defects of his race and time. Aspiring to be the leader of a nation of third-rate men, he had to stoop to the common level. When he struck out for realms above that level he always came to grief: this was the "unsafe" Roosevelt, the Roosevelt who was laughed at, the Roosevelt retired suddenly to cold storage. This was the Roosevelt who, in happier times and a better place, might have been. Well, one does what one can.

The youngest writer in this volume, JOHN BRAEMAN (1932–   ), comes to the Progressive era through a doctoral dissertation of Albert J. Beveridge that currently is being revised for publication. In the article below, a model review essay, Braeman comments on the latest books, calls attention to the diverse aspects of Progressive thought about government and the economy, and asks which aspects are useful today. His is a sober summary of the issues involved in this section of the book. An assistant professor of history at Brooklyn College, Mr. Braeman was born in New York City, attended Harvard and Johns Hopkins, and taught previously at Ohio State University.*

Seven Profiles: Modernists and Traditionalists

A consensus has developed among most historians of the period about the nature of early twentieth-century progressivism. Their typical progressive was a member of the urban middle class, a professional man or independent businessman, comfortable financially, well-educated, a native-born Protestant, probably of New England stock. These men felt themselves overshadowed and threatened by the wealth and power of the new masters of capital, and their progressivism was a reaction to this "status revolution." "Looking backward to an older America," Professor George E. Mowry finds, the progressives hoped "to recapture the older individualistic values in all the strata of political, economic, and social life." "The central fear," declares Professor Richard Hofstadter, "was fear of power," and the progressive movement, "at its heart, was an effort to realize familiar and traditional ideals" that had "taken form under the conditions of a predominantly rural society with a broad diffusion of property and power."[1]

[1] George E. Mowry, *The California Progressives* (Berkeley and Los Angeles, 1951) pp. 86–104; Richard Hofstadter, *The Age of Reform, From Bryan to F.D.R.* (New York, Vintage edition, 1960), pp. 131–148, 215–227; George E. Mowry, *The Era of Theodore Roosevelt, 1900–1912* (New York, 1958), pp. 85–105.

* John Braeman, "Seven Progressives," *Business History Review*, XXXV (Winter 1961), 581–592. Reprinted by permission of the Business History Review.

A reading, however, of the recently published biographies of seven leading Republican progressives[2] raises the question whether such generalizations about the movement are warranted. Even the most cursory glance reveals a split—one noted by contemporaries no less than by subsequent historians—between those progressives who favored accepting, and then regulating, the large corporations and those favoring a return to the old competitive system of small units. Half of the progressives, Theodore Roosevelt lamented in 1911, "are really representative of a kind of rural toryism, which wishes to attempt the impossible task of returning to the economic conditions that obtained sixty years ago. The other half wishes to go forward along the proper lines, that is, to recognize the inevitableness and necessity of combinations in business, and meet it by a corresponding increase in governmental power over big business. . . ."[3]

2 William H. Harbaugh, *Power and Responsibility: The Life and Times of Theodore Roosevelt* (New York, 1961); John A. Garraty, *Righthand Man: The Life of George W. Perkins* (New York, 1961); Elting E. Morison, *Turmoil and Tradition: A Study of the Life and Times of Henry L. Stimson* (Boston, 1960); Charles Forcey, *The Crossroads of Liberalism: Croly, Weyl, Lippmann, and the Progressive Era, 1900–1925* (New York, 1961); M. Nelson McGeary, *Gifford Pinchot: Forester-Politician* (Princeton, 1960); Marian C. McKenna, *Borah* (Ann Arbor, 1961); and Robert M. La Follette, *La Follette's Autobiography* (Madison, 1960). Since *La Follette's Autobiography* ends just before the 1912 election, I have used Belle Case La Follette and Fola La Follette's *Robert M. La Follette* (2 vols.; New York, 1953) for information about his later years. Although Professor Forcey's book is a study of Croly, Weyl, and Lippmann, I have dealt for the purposes of this essay only with Croly as the most important and central figure of the three. All information and quotations in the text are drawn from these above-mentioned works unless otherwise cited.

3 Quoted in Mowry, *The Era of Theodore Roosevelt*, p. 55.

Their preoccupation with domestic politics has blinded most historians to the larger import of this split.[4] But the same line of cleavage can be found in foreign affairs. Those championing regulation of large corporations favored recognition of, and positive action to meet, the international responsibilities incumbent upon the United States as a world power; those looking to restore competition favored the traditional policy of American isolation from active participation in world affairs. This division within the progressive ranks was, I would suggest, a fundamental one. On the one hand were those willing to face without flinching the challenges and dangers of the twentieth century. On the other hand were those who hoped to recapture the small-town, "little" America of the nineteenth century—those whom Roosevelt called "not progressive at all, but retrogressive."

Let us call one group the "moderns"; the other, the "traditionalists." Of our seven progressives, four—George W. Perkins, Henry L. Stimson, Herbert Croly, and Theodore Roosevelt—belonged to the "moderns" camp; two—Robert M. La Follette and William E. Borah—to the "traditionalist" camp. The seventh —Gifford Pinchot—followed a path between the two camps, inspired by the new spirit of the "moderns," yet drawn by the ideas and values of the "traditionalists."

The four "moderns" had similar backgrounds: all were members by birth of

4 William E. Leuchtenburg, "Progressivism and Imperialism: The Progressive Movement and American Foreign Policy, 1898–1916," *Mississippi Valley Historical Review*, vol. XXXIX (Dec., 1952), pp. 483–504, is a valuable pioneering attempt to link up the domestic and foreign aspects of progressivism, but the approach differs from that taken in the present essay.

respectable middle-class America and all were financially comfortable, through inheritance or their own exertions, in their later years. All were by inheritance and conviction Republicans. The G.O.P. had saved the Union; the Democracy was, in the words of the Reverend Samuel D. Burchard, the party of "Rum, Romanism, and Rebellion." All were city-born and city-bred. Although Roosevelt and Stimson were enthusiastic lovers of the outdoor life, and Perkins found fishing his chief relaxation, all looked at American problems through the eyes of city dwellers. Only Roosevelt, of the four, paid much attention to rural problems; but even his major concern was with the social, political, and economic issues arising in a modern and highly industrialized urban society.

All four grew up in strongly religious households, and although none remained in later years more than a formal churchgoer, all retained the ideal of service inculcated during their youth. George Perkins inherited from his father "a stern Presbyterian sense of obligation," which found expression first in the insurance business, then in public service. Henry Stimson grew up in a family whose watchwords were Right, Truth, Duty; took as his youthful ambition "to do good in some way"; and found that the private practice of law failed to satisfy his "ethical side." Herbert Croly reached maturity under the influence of his father's mystical "religion of humanity" with its preachment that the world is to be improved, not simply accepted. Theodore Roosevelt, Sr., transmitted to the future chief executive his own Presbyterian sense of moral duty and habit of *noblesse oblige,* and T.R. himself defined religion "as service to one's fellowmen rendered by following the great rule

of justice and mercy, of wisdom and righteousness."

The central theme in the thought of all four men was *order.* The depression-wracked and crisis-filled years of the 1890's had been a searing experience. The disruptive forces of modern industrialism—the widening extremes of wealth and poverty, the rise of giant corporations, the increasing restiveness of labor, the dread specter of class warfare—had threatened during those years to rend the fabric of society. The danger of fragmentation, of social upheaval, of anarchy, weighed heavily upon the minds of our four "moderns" in the years that followed. Their great preoccupation was stability, order, control. They faced the twentieth century with mingled apprehension and hope—apprehension lest these disruptive forces tear society to pieces; hope that men of intelligence and good will could harness these forces for the general welfare. The crucial problem, Herbert Croly explained, was "of keeping such a highly differentiated society fundamentally whole and sound."

One potential force of disruption was the labor movement. While favoring a judicious mixture of corporate paternalism and welfare legislation to blunt the threat from below, all the "moderns" remained suspicious of organized labor. Stimson denounced the United Mine Workers as an "arrogant minority—challenging the American Republic" and called for incorporation to curb union abuses. Perkins introduced a paternalistic profit-sharing plan at United States Steel, but he would not deal with the workers on equal terms across a bargaining table. Although Roosevelt, in his later years in the White House, came more and more to acknowledge that unions were as necessary and as inevitable as big business, he retained an abiding fear of labor violence, never abandoned his opposition to the closed shop, and remained anxious to guard against possible "abuses" of union power. Even Croly, who called for "substantial discrimination" by the government in behalf of unions, demanded that the government discriminate between "good" and "bad" unions by setting down standards for union behavior.

Far more immediately threatening than the labor movement was the giant corporation—and the threat to American democracy presented by the increasing concentration of economic power in fewer and fewer hands was the foremost problem before the public at the turn of the century. Perkins, Professor Garraty shows, approached this problem from his own experience in business. Competition was cruel, wasteful, and outmoded; the giant combinations of the twentieth century were the inevitable result of modern technology. An admirer of bigness, Perkins believed that large-scale enterprise meant the most efficient use of natural and human resources. But how could such businesses be compelled to live up to their social responsibilities? Although he himself was a man of honor, he knew that many other tycoons were not. Destruction was out of the question; the solution was government regulation —and regulation by the national government, not the states, because business had become nationwide in its scope.

Stimson came to the problem from his experience as United States Attorney for the Southern District of New York. That post, Professor Morison writes, brought him face to face for the first time with what he later termed "the new front of great corporate transgression." As with Perkins, his starting point was that the large corporation was indispensable for industrial progress. On the other hand, he realized that a democracy could not "permit unregulated control over production and sale of its necessities." Again like Perkins, he turned to regulation by the national government to resolve the dilemma. Although he had achieved as District Attorney impressive successes in restraining and punishing corporate wrongdoing, he had no faith in sporadic lawsuits as instruments of regulation. Required was a commission that would provide "for the permanent, continuous and watchful oversight of corporate business engaged in interstate commerce. . . ."

His conclusion was much the same, but the starting point for Herbert Croly was, as Professor Forcey points out, cultural rather than political or economic. Longing to infuse the United States with the communal spirit, the patriotic *élan,* that had nourished the cultural achievements of ancient Greece or Renaissance Italy, he feared lest unrestrained corporate power destroy the national cohesion demanded for creative art. Yet to dismantle the trusts would weaken the nation industrially. His remedy was that the large corporation should be accepted for its benefits, but should be regulated by a strong, centralized government. Under modern conditions, Croly held, the Hamiltonian reliance upon a powerful national government was indispensable for the achievement of Jeffersonian ends, ends which he described as "essentially equalitarian and socialistic."

This approach to the problem of corporate power was given its practical application by Theodore Roosevelt. Professor Harbaugh argues that T.R. was not the sophisticated conservative of John M. Blum's *The Republican Roosevelt,* but was a genuine progressive

moved by the vision of a happier, more
just, and less privileged America. There
is no denying that Roosevelt became
morally indignant at injustice; yet, as
Professor Harbaugh himself concedes, he
generally heard the call of duty only
when victory appeared probable. The
recurring motif in Roosevelt's thought
from the 1890's on was his near-obsessive
fear of upheaval from below. From his
days as governor, he looked to defend a
middle ground against corporate wrongdoing, on the one side, and demagoguery
and mob rule, on the other. Although
wielding the Sherman Act to punish the
most flagrant wrongdoing, he rejected
any large-scale trust-busting as a vain
attempt to turn back the clock. Government regulation encompassing a broad
extension of federal power was his
answer to the dangers from left and
right.

The cry "regulation, not destruction"
was a catchy slogan, but what did it
mean? That depended upon the man,
and the time. For regulation was en-
visaged as a pragmatic way of curbing
abuses without losing the advantages of
large-scale enterprise. George Perkins
favored a federal licensing arrangement.
Stimson wanted legislation that would
prohibit "in detail the various methods
of unfair trade by which competition is
destroyed" along with a permanent
watch-dog agency that would enforce the
law and publicize corporate wrongdoing.
Theodore Roosevelt first backed legislation for compulsory publicity, then led
in pushing through a series of *ad hoc*
regulatory measures designed to meet
specific needs—the Hepburn railroad rate
law, the meat inspection law, and the
pure food and drug act—and at the high
point of his "New Nationalism" declared that in extreme cases the govern-

ment should be empowered to "exercise
control over monopoly prices, as rates on
railroads are now controlled...." Going
further, Herbert Croly called for nationalization of such natural monopolies
as the railroads.

All agreed upon the need for strong
executive leadership, and further agreed
that this leadership must be impartial
among the contending interests in
society. But none faced squarely the
question of how such powerful admini-
strators could be kept responsible to the
public at large. They defined the problem in terms of individual character, and
their own high sense of personal
righteousness blinded them to the dangers of unrestrained power. Perkins'
behavior in the management of the New
York Life Insurance Company was a case
in point. Believing himself an honest
man, he paid scant attention to legal
technicalities. Such restrictions, he, in
effect, told the Armstrong Committee
investigators, applied only to those who
were dishonest. Although Theodore
Roosevelt in his heyday as a Bull Mooser
came out for the initiative, referendum,
and even limited recall of judicial decisions, he chafed throughout his life
against restraints upon his power—and
marred his record with such willful and
irresponsible assertions of ego as the
Panama episode or his criminal libel suit
against the New York *World*.

The legal-minded Stimson was more
aware of the dangers involved. He
advocated a clear-cut definition of governmental responsibility to reduce corruption, log-rolling, and inefficiency. When
T.R. came out for the recall of judicial
decisions, he reaffirmed his devotion to
an independent judiciary as a bulwark
against the misuse of authority. But, in
the end, he, too, placed his reliance upon

individual character—he and his friends were honorable men, and honorable men would not betray their trust. The most intellectually perceptive of the group, Croly saw to the heart of the dilemma involved in reconciling his demand for strong executive leadership with democracy. Yet he evaded, rather than answered, the problem. Even while advocating the referendum and recall, he took refuge in what Professor Forcey calls his latent mysticism. The final triumph of reform, he confessed, would have to wait for some "national reformer in the guise of Saint Michael" or "some democratic Saint Francis . . . some imitator of Christ" to lead America to "national regeneration."

These progressives could shelve the problem the more easily because of their middle-class bias. They looked for leadership of the reform movement not to the extremely wealthy—although an occasional public-spirited and farsighted millionaire such as George Perkins would lend a hand—nor to the very poor, but to the God-fearing, liberty-loving middle class. Their reliance upon the middle class as the fulcrum of progress rested upon the faith that gradual and limited reform could meet the dangers facing the republic. They desired no fundamental alteration in the structure of American society. The problems of the modern age, Roosevelt declared at the beginning of his second term, called for the same qualities that had distinguished the American people in past crises, qualities not lost in the present generation—those "of practical intelligence, courage, or hardihood, and endurance, and above all the power of devotion to a lofty ideal."

While grappling with the problems of a modern industrialized society, the "moderns" faced boldly the responsibilities imposed by America's new position as a world power. Inspired by a mixture of humanitarian zeal with desire for foreign markets to absorb the surplus of farm and factory, Perkins, Stimson, and Roosevelt hailed the burst of overseas expansion at the turn of the century. Despite his misgivings about the bloodshed in subjugating the Philippines, even Croly welcomed the imperialist surge as awakening the republic to its new duties. More significant is that Stimson, Croly, and Roosevelt stood convinced that a German victory in World War I would menace the security of the United States. The important point is not so much the correctness of their diagnosis—that is debatable; but that unlike most of their fellow Americans, they realized that isolation was no longer possible, that the free security afforded by the ocean and the British navy was drawing to a close, that the outcome of a far-off war might have grave consequences for this country.

The most sophisticated proponent of this approach was Herbert Croly. The revolution in technology and communications, Croly believed, had made isolation impossible. The United States needed a positive foreign policy to promote its "national interest." That national interest was world peace. But world peace could not be secured by mere pronunciamentos. It could be secured only by a judicious use of American power. The chief exponent in action of this strategy was Theodore Roosevelt. Exercising to the full the chief executive's control over foreign affairs, T.R. sounded the death-knell of the old isolationism and made the United States a force to be reckoned with in the power struggles of Europe and the Far East. Despite his fervent nationalism, he took limited, but still precedent-shattering, steps toward international cooperation. He even maintained before his death what Professor Harbaugh calls a "cautiously affirmative attitude" toward the League of Nations.

T.R. obscured the full significance of his achievements by his raucous jingoism, his contempt for backward nations, and his romantic notions of national honor and war. More successful in awakening the American people to the demands of a realistic foreign policy was Henry L. Stimson. His experience as Secretary of State, Professor Morison concludes, confirmed for Stimson the truth of the Rooseveltian dictum about speaking softly and carrying a big stick. Shackled by the unwillingness of President Herbert Hoover, and the public at large, to back a meaningful effort, individual or collective, to restrain Japanese aggression in Manchuria, he learned firsthand the futility of moral stands unbacked by force. Throughout the 1930's, Stimson warned that isolation was impossible under modern conditions. Before most of his fellow countrymen, he saw the Axis threat to the nation's security and warned against the isolationist fallacy that the United States could stand apart from the rest of the world. A realist to the last, he foresaw that the United Nations could not succeed unless the big powers settled their differences beforehand.

In many ways, Gifford Pinchot belonged to the "moderns." He was, as Professor McGeary relates, an Easterner, born to wealth, Yale-educated, well-traveled. He grew up in a strongly religious atmosphere and imbibed the same moral fervor to do good. He shared the prevailing faith in moral character— a belief which in regard to his own

behavior made for a self-righteousness that stigmatized any opposition as villainous and dishonest. During World War I, he displayed a similar pro-Allied bias and distrust of German ambitions, and in the years before America's entry into World War II, joined his friend Henry Stimson in warning that the United States could not safely sit by while the European democracies went under. He wrote T.R.'s famous Ossawatomie speech in which the former chief executive called for a strong, centralized national state to direct the country's economic life; he himself was a staunch supporter of government regulation of railroads and natural resources; and in his most radical phase, in 1913 and 1914, even favored government ownership.

His passion for orderly development appeared most graphically in his leadership of the conservation movement. From one point of view, the conservation movement can be regarded, as Professor Samuel Hays has contended,[5] as primarily a scientific movement concerned with rational planning to promote the efficient development and use of natural resources. There is no gainsaying that the conservation movement was a reaction against the undirected and wasteful exploitation of resources under the old individualistic dispensation. The conservationists did struggle to replace the philosophy of "grab and grasp" with a scientifically worked-out, long-range program—did, in short, seek to apply the advantages of organization and planning to the problem of resources management—and it was this side of the movement that attracted the support of the large cattle and lumber interests.

[5] Samuel P. Hays, *Conservation and the Gospel of Efficiency: The Progressive Conservation Movement, 1890–1920* (Cambridge, 1959), especially pp. 261–276.

Yet it would be an error to assume that the democratic, antimonopolistic slogans that accompanied the movement[6] were mere window dressing to win votes. The truth is that Pinchot looked back nostalgically to the older America of the small holder. This nostalgia was reflected in his concern for the problems of rural life, his blasts against monopoly, his repeated claims that he was fighting for the little man against the big man, his denunciations of special privilege and calls for the restoration of equality of opportunity, and his leadership of the fight within the Progressive Party for a plank demanding strengthening of the Sherman Act. His good fortune was that in the conservation movement he could fulfill his passion for scientific planning while appearing to promote democratic equalitarianism.

Such good fortune was not the lot of Borah and La Follette. They had to deal with a broader range of questions, and the gap between their remedies and the realities of modern life became painfully apparent—most painfully so in the case of Borah, who lived past most of his generation, until the end of the 1930's. Both were poor farm boys; both struggled against heavy odds for an education; both made their marks as lawyers in small towns. But not so much background as ideology made the crucial difference. Albert J. Beveridge shared much the same background—although Indianapolis was a larger, more highly industrialized urban center than Boise or Madison—but belonged ideologically to the "moderns." [7] La Follette and Borah shared a common loyalty to the vision of the older, individualistic America of the nineteenth century, and this loyalty shaped their policies, domestic and foreign.

To place La Follette in the same category with Borah is in many ways unfair to the Wisconsin reformer. La Follette had broader and more humane sympathies; he had a deeper and more genuine passion for social justice. Not only did he support welfare legislation on behalf of working men and women—much of which Borah also supported—but he displayed more sympathy for the aspirations of organized labor. Whereas La Follette favored exempting unions from prosecution under the antitrust laws, Borah's early brushes with the violent and turbulent Western Miners Federation left him with an abiding distrust of unbridled union power. Not so dogmatically wedded to states' rights, limited-government notions as his Idaho colleague, La Follette was willing to sanction so far-reaching an extension of federal power as that involved in the child labor amendment to achieve a desired reform. Again unlike Borah, he broadened his devotion to democracy to include women as well as men.

Most striking is the difference in their achievements. No important congressional measure bears Borah's name; he was responsible for no major administrative policy. He was a gadfly, a dissenter, and, in the eyes of many, a wrecker. La Follette, on the contrary, left behind a record of positive accomplishment in his home state that made Wisconsin famous as "the laboratory of democracy." Even in the more hostile atmosphere of the Senate, his constructive work continued—the Seamen's Act of 1915 was but one testimonial to his parliamentary skill. A man

[6] This aspect of the conservation movement is emphasized in J. Leonard Bates, "Fulfilling American Democracy: The Conservation Movement, 1907–1921," *Mississippi Valley Historical Review*, vol. XLIV (June, 1957), pp. 29–57.

[7] John Braeman, "Albert J. Beveridge and the New Nationalism" (Ph.D. Thesis, Johns Hopkins University, 1960).

of firsthand experience in practical administrative problems, he understood the importance of technical expertise in dealing with complex economic problems. Perhaps more than any other man, he pioneered in the use of expert commissions in the work of government. Yet notwithstanding these differences, Borah and La Follette shared much the same world view—a world view based upon the vision of an innocent republic of happy artisans, prosperous yeomen, and thriving small business safe behind the impassable ocean from the crimes and follies of the Old World.

They could not miss the gulf between reality and this vision. To explain what had happened, they had recourse to a conspiracy theory. La Follette's autobiography is filled with denunciations of the secret and corrupt means by which the forces of special privilege have perverted the democratic process for their private gain. Borah's fulminations against eastern bankers and speculators reflected the same temper of mind. Their approach to foreign affairs displayed the same limitations. Reflecting the anti-British animus lingering on in rural America from the days of Populism, both men feared lest this country fall prey to the diplomatic wiles of perfidious Albion. Like most of the antiwar progressives, La Follette blamed eastern financiers and munitions makers for pushing the United States into World War I to safeguard their loans to the Allies. Although voting for the war resolution—an action he later regretted— Borah denounced as bankers' plots the League of Nations, the Four Power Pact of the Washington Conference, and the repeal of the arms embargo.

The reverse side of this conspiracy theory was their faith in the wisdom and righteousness of the people. The need was to remove the barriers of caucus and convention that kept the people from a direct voice in affairs and allowed selfish manipulators to pervert the democratic process. Both men made the direct popular primary a key plank in their platforms, and with the primary achieved, both built unbeatable personal followings in their home states. More democracy all along the line was their remedy for the nation's ills. The masses were fundamentally peace-loving; a popular referendum on war, therefore, would safeguard the country against foreign intrigues. The people were sound at heart; given the direct primary, they would "send honest men to Washington." And with honest men in office, La Follette prophesied, "all our problems, however complex, will be easily solved."

The first step in solving those problems would be to halt the trend to bigness in industry, to reverse the tempo of consolidation, by vigorous enforcement of the Sherman Anti-Trust law. If Roosevelt had vigorously enforced that law, La Follette charged, he could have routed the few trusts then in existence at the start of his presidency. But his inaction allowed consolidation to continue apace. Yet time still remained, the Wisconsin senator believed, in which to recover lost ground if the Sherman Act were strengthened. The major plank in his 1924 race for the presidency was his pledge to uproot monopoly; that, the platform declared, was "the great issue before the American people." [8] Borah was another advocate of strengthening the Sherman Act. Voting against the Federal Trade Commission bill, the Idaho lawmaker called for the destruction of trusts and monopolies, not their regulation. Unless monopolies were

8 Kenneth C. MacKay, *The Progressive Movement of 1924* (New York, 1947), p. 11.

destroyed, he warned, the independent small businessman—the backbone of the republic—would be no more.

Yet both men remained wedded to the dream of material progress. A case in point was Borah's hostility to the conservation movement as hindering the rapid development of Idaho. More striking was both men's ambivalent stand upon the tariff. The guiding principle in their approach to the tariff appeared to be whose ox was being gored. In the fight over the Payne-Aldrich tariff, Borah voted with the regulars in return for the protection of hides and timber demanded by his constituents. His opposition to subsequent tariff legislation ranging from Canadian reciprocity to the Hawley-Smoot tariff reflected his conviction that these measures were unfair to the agricultural interests; but withal he continued a staunch believer in protection. La Follette's bitter opposition to Canadian reciprocity testified to his concern for Wisconsin's farmers. And La Follette, too, though a biting critic of tariff abuses, reaffirmed in his autobiography the Whiggish vision of a flourishing home market benefiting farmer, laborer, and manufacturer.

Their ambivalence toward the successful businessman as a cultural hero made for an irreconcilable confusion of purposes. In the chapter in his autobiography entitled "Progressive Government Produces Business Prosperity," La Follette explained that his purpose "was not to 'smash' corporations," but to root out special "privileges, unfair advantages, and political corruption." "Where these do not exist," he declared, "the object has been to foster and encourage business activity." But the Wisconsin lawmaker, like so many of his contemporaries, never succeeded in explaining how he would break up the trusts without smashing corporations. It is noteworthy that the Wilson administration, pledged to destroy monopoly and restore competition, turned to the New Nationalist's program of regulation when in office.[9] It is even more noteworthy that, with the passage of time, Borah's attacks on monopoly became sheer bombast alternating with denunciations of the New Deal's tentative steps toward government planning as threatening constitutional government.

The same nostalgia for an older America shaped both men's foreign policy. At the turn of the century, both were ardent supporters of overseas expansion. Although they retained some of their earlier jingoism—La Follette, for instance, opposed the Wilson administration's repeal of the Panama Canal Tolls Act, while Borah denounced what he called Wilson's "peace at any price" policy toward Mexico—in later years both took anti-imperialist stands. La Follette attacked the President's handling of the Vera Cruz incident and introduced a resolution disavowing any annexationist designs against Mexico; he was sympathetic to the aspirations of underdeveloped countries for freedom; and he favored recognition of the Soviet Union.[10] Borah was even more vocal: he assailed American intervention during the 1920's in the Caribbean; he supported a peaceful settlement with Mexico over the nationalization of American property; he strove to align the United States with the Chinese revolution; and he backed recognition of the Soviet Union.

[9] Arthur S. Link, *Woodrow Wilson and the Progressive Era, 1910–1917* (New York, 1954), pp. 66–80.

[10] Valuable for tracing La Follette's shift from imperialism to anti-imperialism is Padraic C. Kennedy, "La Follette's Imperialist Flirtation," *Pacific Historical Review,* vol. XXIX (May, 1960), pp. 131–144.

All this has the appearance of modernity and foresight; but a different picture emerges when we look beneath the surface and examine the bases of their foreign policy. The distrust both men felt for the bankers and large industrialists within the United States was reflected in their distaste for "dollar diplomacy." But this distaste was reinforced by their indifference to the strategic implications of the international power struggle. Neither man had a sophisticated understanding of the importance of force in international relations. Their reliance upon what Borah termed "the impelling power of enlightened public opinion" to restrain aggression was an index of their illusions in this sphere. Their naïveté reflected the limitations imposed by their nostalgia for the past—was the product, in short, of their refusal to accept the reality that the United States was inextricably and inevitably part of a larger world system.

The proof was not their opposition to American intervention in World War I; the case can be argued that a German victory would not have menaced the nation's security. Nor was the crux of the matter their opposition to the Treaty of Versailles; so ardent an internationalist as Herbert Croly joined in denouncing the pact as an unjust peace containing the seeds of future wars. What is damning was the underlying assumptions governing their behavior. Europe, La Follette warned in the hectic days preceding America's entry into World War I, was "cursed with a contagious, ... deadly plague, whose spread threatens to devastate the civilized world." Regardless of "material loss, or commercial inconvenience," the United States should "keep [its] people at home" and "quarantine against it." Assailing the

postwar Four Power Pact, the Wisconsin lawmaker declared that "we can only serve the world and our own people while we are free to pursue our own ideals and our own ambitions in an effort to uphold freedom and democracy and the rights of the common man."

The same impulse motivated Borah. He believed, writes his biographer, "that Europe has a set of primary interests wholly different from ours. . . ." For all his insight into the economic interdependence of nations, he continued to preach that the greatest service that the United States could perform for the world, as for itself, was to maintain its democratic way of life pure and unsullied by foreign contamination. He feared, Miss McKenna concludes, lest this country "risk a compromise of its faith and a coarsening of its character by active entanglement with the Old World." These romantic prepossessions inspired his opposition to the Four Power Pact as an insidious alliance that would ensnare the United States in alien conflicts; sparked his fight against this country's joining the World Court; and culminated in his quixotic crusade to outlaw war.

No one can know how La Follette would have reacted to the domestic and foreign crises of the 1930's. Perhaps his passion for social justice and pragmatic temper of mind would have led him to support the far-reaching extension of the power of the federal government involved in the New Deal. Perhaps his humanitarianism and love of freedom would have awakened him to the threat posed by the fascist dictatorships to American democracy and brought him to support measures for collective security against aggression. The careers of his sons and political heirs indicate that the first possibility was more probable than the second.[11] Borah lived long enough to go publicly on record, and that record, as set forth in detail by Miss McKenna, gives eloquent testimony to the dangers of good will undirected by an informed intelligence.

Though sympathetic to the liberal aspirations of the New Deal, he assailed one after another of the measures taken to implement these aims—the N.R.A., the Hull reciprocal trade program, the administration's monetary policy, the A.A.A. He was appalled by the resulting centralization of power in Washington, and before long was denouncing the New Deal as a threat to constitutional government. In foreign affairs, he worked to rally a new "battalion of death" to check the "foreign ambitions" of F.D.R.; he refused to condemn or even protest the aggressive steps taken by Hitler; he scoffed at the dangers of a European war and told Secretary Hull that his sources of information were more reliable than the State Department's; and even after the war broke out, he led the fight to block repeal of the arms embargo. To his dying day, he held firmly to his belief that this country should remain aloof from the European conflict even if that meant a Nazi victory and should rely only on its own resources for national security. The Second World War and its aftermath shattered beyond repair the illusions that had sustained Borah along with so many of his fellow Americans.

This line of cleavage between what I have called the "traditionalists" and "moderns" is, I would reiterate, funda-

[11] Edward N. Doan, *The La Follettes and the Wisconsin Idea* (New York and Toronto, 1947), pp. 143–297.

mental to understanding the progressive movement as a whole. Yet as important as these differences were, the historian should remember that all these men were children of the same age and shared certain basic attitudes and assumptions. All accepted the certainty and universality of the Victorian code of morality. The words "truth," "honor," "justice," and "patriotism" had a real meaning. Even that philosophical relativist, Herbert Croly, snuck the absolutes of his father's "religion of humanity" through the back door. The progressive movement was as much a moral crusade as a political and economic movement—and it was a moral crusade that at times took strange twists. Borah and Pinchot, for instance, were both ardent prohibitionists.

Along with this concern for moral uplift came a belief in progress. Progress was no longer automatic; but all the progressives believed that men, through the exercise of intelligence and will, could master events, not be their slaves; that society could move itself forward; that the United States could solve the problems of a modern industrial society without doing violence to its democratic institutions. The third major belief was that the United States constituted God's favored people. All, whether internationalists such as Croly or isolationists such as Borah, believed that this country was made of different coin from the rest of the world and had a special mission to perform. These articles of faith gave to the men of the progressive era a drive, a verve, and an optimism to which we of a more tired, disillusioned, and cynical generation can only look back with a certain nostalgia of our own.

WILLIAM E. LEUCHTENBURG (1922–   ), a specialist in twentieth-century American history, shares some of the doubts of his Columbia University colleague Richard Hofstadter about the modernity of the Progressive era. In his sprightly book on the 1920s, from which a chapter is reproduced here, Professor Leuchtenburg asks why the Progressive era gave way to the age of normalcy. His answer, that Progressivism contributed to its own demise and therefore prepared the ground for a "botched civilization," contradicts Parrington's opening statement of this book.*

► ## Tired Radicals

In 1914 the progressive movement had reached its zenith. Two years before, the country had been aroused by a four-party contest in which the conservative Republican incumbent, William Howard Taft, had been overwhelmed by his progressive rivals; Woodrow Wilson, the Democratic spokesman for the New Freedom, had ousted Taft from the White House, while Teddy Roosevelt, the Progressive party candidate, had run a strong second. Even Taft, who in 1912 carried only two states in the Electoral College, had established a record as a reformer in office—particularly by a vigorous prosecution of trusts—that

would have seemed unbelievable a short time before. Most startling of all, Eugene Debs, the Socialist candidate, had polled almost a million votes. Wilson in office had proceeded to carry out the mandate for the New Freedom, driving through Congress an impressive number of reforms. In 1914 progressivism was triumphant; six years later it was apparently dead as a doornail, buried under the Harding landslide. What killed progressivism?

The most obvious answer was that progressivism had been killed by the war. In 1912, when social reform was at floodtide, the chief leaders of the move-

---

* Reprinted from *The Perils of Prosperity* by William E. Leuchtenburg by permission of the University of Chicago Press. © 1958 by The University of Chicago.

ment were Roosevelt, Wilson, La Follette, Bryan, and Debs. By 1920, these
leaders and their followers were snarling
enemies, hopelessly divided by the issues
of the war. Bryan had resigned from
Wilson's cabinet, to be met by a tirade
of abuse from Wilson's supporters, and,
although there was a temporary recon-
ciliation in 1916, he was an outspoken
opponent of Wilson's strategy on the
League three years later. Roosevelt's
supporters viewed Wilson and La Follette with the angry contempt usually
reserved for traitors. Roosevelt himself
had denounced La Follette as a "hun
within our gates" and "the most sinister
enemy of democracy in America." Wilson kept Debs in a federal prison, and
Debs scornfully dismissed Wilson as "the
most pathetic figure in the world."

Nothing reveals the damage the war
did in splitting the ranks of the progressives so much as the progressive attitude
toward La Follette. No man in America
had done more to advance the cause of
social reform than "Battle Bob." As
governor of Wisconsin, he found the
state a corporation barony and, working
with a group of university professors,
transformed it into the model social
laboratory of the nation. Elected to the
Senate in 1905, he quickly became the
recognized leader of the progressive
forces fighting for railroad legislation,
conservation, and protection for labor.
But once he came out in opposition to
entrance in the war—he denounced it as
a plot of profiteers and protested that
"the poor who are called to rot in the
trenches have no organized voice"—none
of this counted. The muckraker Charles
Edward Russell execrated him as a
"traitor in disguise" who was doing "the
dirty work of the Kaiser"; La Follette,
he declared, was "a big yellow streak."

During the war, La Follette's old allies,
President Van Hise of the University of
Wisconsin, John Commons, Richard Ely,
and E. A. Ross signed a statement cen-
suring him for disloyalty, while Ely
wrote that La Follette had been "of
more help to the Kaiser than a quarter
of a million troops."

There had long been a close tie between progressivism and nationalism,
particularly among the followers of
Theodore Roosevelt who, not unlike
Joseph Chamberlain in England or, to
a degree, Bismarck in Germany, stood
for a strong state with a sense both of
social obligation and of imperial mission. After their defeat in 1912, Roosevelt and his followers emphasized the
nationalist strain in progressivism, re-
buking Wilson for failing to uphold national honor, first in Latin America, then
in Europe. As leaders of the Progressive
party concentrated their fire on Wilson's
foreign policy, they became more and
more chauvinistic and less and less interested in domestic reform. In December, 1914, the Progressives issued a statement which ignored the reform planks
of their 1912 platform and centered on
a demand for a higher protective tariff.
In January, 1916, the Progressive National Committee denounced Wilson for
failing "to deal adequately with the National honor and industrial welfare" and
called for "a reawakening of our elder
Americanism, of our belief in those
things that our country and our flag
stands for."

Roosevelt himself gave up on progressivism and turned to preparedness and
war. He not only refused to run on the
Progressive ticket in 1916 but urged both
the Progressives and Republicans to
nominate the bleakly conservative Henry
Cabot Lodge as a man of "the broadest

national spirit," who, Roosevelt told the stunned Progressives, was one of the "staunchest fighters for different measures of economic reform in the direction of justice." The Progressive platform of 1916 was indistinguishable from that of the Republicans, which, as the *New Republic* observed, was a "stupidly, defiantly and cynically reactionary document." When the Republicans nominated Hughes, the Progressives indorsed him too, on the grounds that only he could "serve the two vital causes of Americanism and Preparedness." The 1916 campaign marked the end of the Progressive party.

In 1912 the Progressives had been militant crusaders against reaction. As Roosevelt and the Progressives merged with the Republicans on nationalist grounds, they adopted the social ideology of the Old Guard too. In September, 1915, Roosevelt decried the "policy of harassing and jeopardizing business"; six months later he warned that commissions must stand "unflinchingly against any popular clamor which prevents the corporation from getting ample profit." Senator Beveridge, who had a distinguished record as a reformer and especially as a fighter for child labor laws, became a bitter foe of organized labor, attacked the income tax and called for a sales tax, and protested against "persecuting" businessmen. (The Indianapolis Associated Employers, Beveridge wrote enthusiastically, had been highly successful "in the suppression of strikes by force.") In 1918 Roosevelt urged the election to the Senate of four reactionaries, including Albert Fall of New Mexico. "To a peculiar degree," wrote Roosevelt, "Fall embodies the best American Spirit." Delighted by the victories of Fall and other deep-dyed conserva-

tives, Roosevelt was dismayed only by the fact that George Norris and Robert La Follette were needed to form the new Republican majority in the Senate.

The fight over the League and the ugly events of 1919 dealt bruising blows to progressivism. In 1916, Wilson, as spokesman for the progressive wing of the Democratic party, won over a large section of the Progressives, disgusted with Roosevelt's indorsement of Lodge and attracted by Wilsonian reforms, as well as many Socialists and independent social reformers and intellectuals. By 1920, they had turned against Wilson, convinced that he had cynically betrayed democratic ideals at Versailles and that he had stamped out dissent at home. Heralded as the hope of the age, Wilson, in Amos Pinchot's words, put "his enemies in office and his friends in jail." Intellectuals who, as Joseph Freeman wrote, had a sense of "craft solidarity . . . with the professor in the White House," now felt distrustful of all exhorters, teachers, soothsayers, and statesmen. Leery of political messiahs, they approach politics with a new wariness. Herbert Croly spelled out the credo of the postwar liberal: "No more dashes into the political jungle. No more intervention without reservations, without understanding and without specific and intelligent political preparation."

In 1913 progressive intellectuals were giving the United States its first intelligent analysis of modern society and blueprinting an ebullient, buoyantly hopeful program of reform. By 1919 they were a disenchanted lot; discouraged by the war and the peace that followed, they had become, as Walter Weyl wrote, "tired radicals." "The chief distinguishing aspect of the Presidential campaign of 1920," wrote Herbert Croly in the

New Republic, "is the eclipse of liberalism or progressivism as an effective force in American politics." Faced by the victory of political reaction and the disappointment of their hopes for a new international order, they felt an overwhelming sense of their own impotence. Society seemed infinitely less malleable than it once had; they were no longer certain of their ability to shape institutions to their own desires. The man "who aspired to overturn Society," wrote Weyl, "ends by fighting in a dull Board of Directors of a village library for the inclusion of certain books."

Having lost faith in progress, in the rationality and disinterestedness of man, and in the malleability of society, the intellectuals could no longer retain faith in the prewar political solutions. Croly turned from political problems to religious ones, from the problem of changing society to the quest for individual regeneration, and Walter Lippmann attempted to work out a naturalistic ethics. The disillusionment also strengthened the elitist strain in the progressive intellectuals. Since things had turned out so badly, men like Lippmann concluded not that their analyses were mistaken and their assumptions unrealistic but that the people had failed them. In *Public Opinion* (1922), Lippmann emphasized the irrationality of decision-making in politics and argued that men viewed reality in "stereotypes"; in *The Phantom Public* (1925), he attacked the idea that "the compounding of individual ignorances in masses of people can produce a continuous directing force in public affairs" and urged less power for the people and more for an elite class of experts. The former muckraker Lincoln Steffens gave up on parliamentary democracy entirely ("I can't see why everybody is so anxious to save this rotten civilization of ours") and became a warm admirer of Lenin and Mussolini. There was much more *élan* among the intellectuals who hoped to apply science to politics—John Dewey, Charles Beard, Thorstein Veblen—but they talked a good deal about method and not at all about concrete political proposals.

The war and its aftermath played a major part in the transition from the reform atmosphere of the prewar years to the conservative spirit of the 1920's, but too much can be charged to this alone. Much of the explanation of the change lies in the nature of progressivism itself. There was a considerable area of ideological agreement between prewar progressivism and the acquisitive aspirations of the Coolidge era. When Woodrow Wilson declared he was fighting for "the man on the make," when he cried, "just let some of the youngsters I know have a chance and they'll give these gentlemen points," he was talking the language of the businessman. Many of the progressives, especially the Wilsonians, had no trouble adapting themselves to the Coolidge era; such men as Newton Baker and Joe Tumulty surrendered their interest in social reform and found lucrative jobs with oil companies and private utilities in the 1920's. Businessmen, who formed the core of reform groups in many American cities, were excited by the possibilities of the "new" capitalism. As part of a new managerial class with professional aspirations, they made an easy transition from their prewar interest in "efficiency" in government to the postwar emphasis on scientific management and factory welfare programs. A middle-class movement hostile to interest-group politics, progressivism was shocked by the militancy of labor in 1919, and many progressives aligned themselves with property-conscious conservatives. The very men who voted for Wilson and Roosevelt in 1912 flocked to the polls to give landslide majorities to Harding and Coolidge.

Despite the loud clamor against the trusts, progressivism had always been less an economic movement than one of moral reform, and progressivism faded in the 1920's in part because it had succeeded too well. Women's suffrage had been a long-time goal, and prohibition and immigration restriction, while they do not seem "progressive" to a New Deal liberal, were important aims of the prewar progressive. A blend of economic and moral concerns, progressivism in the 1920's tended to concentrate almost wholly on these "moral" issues, although not without some uneasiness over what it had wrought. Prohibition, observes Richard Hofstadter, "was the skeleton at the feast, a grim reminder of the moral frenzy that so many wished to forget, a ludicrous caricature of the reforming impulse, of the Yankee-Protestant notion that it is both possible and desirable to moralize private life through public action." When the immigration-restriction law passed the Senate in 1924, not a single progressive opposed it, and even men like George Norris voted in its favor.

Without a solid labor base, progressivism had little hope for success in the 1920's, but the "moral" issues diverted white, old-stock workers, the backbone of the AF of L craft unions, from economic issues. In 1924, when the Ku Klux Klan, a hooded order which was anti-Catholic, anti-Semitic, anti-Negro, and anti-foreigner, reached the height of popularity, William Allen White ran for governor of Kansas. He decided to be a candidate, he explained, because "the way the Catholics and Jews and colored people were persecuted by the Klan in Kansas was a dirty shame, and I couldn't rest under it." After his defeat he wrote, "Here was a funny thing: labor in the Middle West is shot through with the Ku-Klux Klan. It voted for Coolidge . . . because he was right on the Pope. I didn't get much of it because I was wrong on the Pope. . . . Certainly nothing has hit labor such a smash in my memory in politics as the Ku-Klux Klan. . . . It will be a decade before labor recovers what it has lost by flirting with the Ku-Klux Klan."

American radicalism was almost defunct in the 1920's. Prosecution during the war cut IWW membership in half; government raids in the Red Scare and defection of "Wobbly" leaders to the Communists decimated the remainder. The Palmer raids almost wiped out the Communists by cutting the membership of the two Communist parties at least four-fifths. (Ironically, by driving the Communists underground, the government strengthened the conspiratorial sense of the Slavic groups, who fancied themselves as being in the same position as the Bolsheviks under the Czar.) By 1920 there were only 8,000 to 15,000 Communists in the United States (the actual count is probably much closer to the lower figure), of whom only 1,000 to 2,000 were English-speaking. The Socialist party went rapidly downhill. In 1920 Eugene Debs, prisoner 9653 at the Atlanta federal penitentiary, won 900,000 votes on the Socialist ticket, but this was a much smaller percentage than he had received in 1912. In that banner year of socialism, the party had 118,000 members; ten years later, in 1922, it had only 11,000. In some states the Socialists virtually disappeared. In Oklahoma, the leading Socialist state in the country in 1914, where merchants had displayed the red flag in their store windows as a commercial expedient, the socialist party claimed only 14 members in 1924.

In the Great Plains states, the historic home of populism and Republican insurgency, progressivism continued to thrive. In 1915 the former Socialist A. C. Townley organized the Nonpartisan League in the heavily rural state of North Dakota. Finding the wheat farmers chafing under a government subservient to the millers of Minneapolis and St. Paul, Townley urged them to take the state away from the "sleek, smooth-tongued, bay-windowed fellows that looked well, talked well, lived well, lied well." In 1916 the League elected an obscure farmer to the governorship of North Dakota, and in the next few years it spread through the wheat belt from Minnesota to Washington. With a program that Thorstein Veblen labeled "agrarian syndicalism," the League in North Dakota created a state bank, a state grain elevator, a state flour mill, a compulsory hail insurance fund, and public low-cost housing for farmers and workers. In South Dakota the League added a state cement plant and a state-owned coal mine.

Elsewhere, however, the League was never able to match the success it had in the wheat area tapped by the Twin Cities. Harried as unpatriotic for its coolness or actual opposition to American participation in World War I, the League was crushed by a critical fall in farm prices in 1921. The state bank and many other state projects ran into financial difficulty, and the League discovered that so long as a state was dependent on Minneapolis or Chicago capital, it could not carry on socialistic experiments even within its borders. By 1922 the League was moribund.

Since the League's program was not narrowly agrarian, it was able to combine with trade unions in a farmer-labor political movement. In Minnesota it laid the foundations for an enduring tradition of farmer-labor unity, but outside the wheat belt farmers were more skeptical about farmer-labor cooperation. The more prosperous corn-belt farmers were more likely to view labor unions as enemies rather than allies. When Samuel Gompers called for farmer-labor unity in June, 1921, the farm journal editor Henry Wallace, later to be Franklin Roosevelt's Secretary of Agriculture, replied: "The fact is that the farmers are suffering more now from the leaders of labor than from the leaders of industry or finance." He lectured Gompers to urge union labor to reduce "exorbitantly high wages" as "an evidence of good faith."

In the face of all these handicaps, what is striking is not the weakness of progressivism but its strength. Through much of the period, the progressives in Congress held the balance of power, and were able to stave off conservative Republican attempts to enact special-interest legislation. In the early years, the progressives were even able to pass legislation of their own. The Esch-Cummins Act of 1920, although a compromise measure, placed railroads under virtually complete federal control, while the Water Power Act of 1920, although it proved ineffective, marked the beginning of federal regulation of electric utilities. In the Harding administration, farm interests won the greatest amount of legislation Congress had ever passed.

Most impressively, from 1921 to 1925 Senator George Norris almost single-handedly and by brilliant legislative legerdemain stopped the Harding and Coolidge administrations from turning the power site at Muscle Shoals in the Tennessee Valley over to private interests. By 1928 Norris had won enough congressional support to turn the tide and throw the private utilities on the defensive. Congress twice passed bills for an ambitious government development of the valley; frustrated both times by presidential vetoes, the campaign that would result in the creation of the Tennessee Valley Authority was, by the end of the Republican era, near success.

The progressives came back from their smashing defeat in 1920 to scare the daylights of the Old Guard in the 1922 elections. In 1920 the Wilson administration had suddenly reduced spending, ended loans to Europe, and raised taxes; the postwar boom was quickly punctured, prices broke violently, and by 1921 the country faced a serious depression. In a single year, America's foreign trade was cut in half and farm prices plummeted. Desperate farmers, not knowing where to turn, used whatever weapon they could improvise. In the cotton belt, night riders burned cotton gins when owners failed to heed warnings not to buy cotton, and in a vain effort to push up prices masked riders in Kentucky cautioned farmers not to send their tobacco to market. In the 1922 elections, farmers resorted to the ballot; progressive Republicans upended Old Guard leaders in the midwestern farm states. In Iowa, irate farmers elected Smith Wildman Brookhart to the Senate; in Wisconsin, La Follette was returned with a 300,000-vote margin; in Minnesota, a Farmer-Labor candidate ousted Senator Frank Kellogg. Even in the East, the Harding forces met defeat. In the Old

Guard stronghold of Pennsylvania, Gifford Pinchot, the leading conservationist of the Progressive era, defeated a reactionary candidate in the Republican gubernatorial primary. "Yesterday," said Senator Moses on hearing the news, "was a bad day for us Tories."

By 1923 midwestern progressives from the farm belt, despairing of both major parties, were talking of launching a national third party in 1924, and they had considerable support among a segment of middle-class intellectuals and reformers and from the Socialist party. The one stumbling block to a third-party move was the hesitancy of organized labor. The powerful railroad unions, infuriated by Harding's support of anti-labor forces, had decided on political action against the Republicans. Rather than run a third ticket they preferred to support the Democrat, William McAdoo, who had won their favor by his operation of the railroads during the war. When, however, it was revealed that McAdoo had been employed as counsel by the oil tycoon, Edwin Doheny, at an annual retainer of $50,000, the unions threw over McAdoo, gave up on the Democratic party, and consented to support an independent ticket in 1924.

The Progressive convention of 1924 in Cleveland had much the same spirit of evangelical revivalism that had characterized the 1912 convention of the earlier Progressives. To the convention came veterans of old protest parties: General Jacob Coxey; the New Jersey editor John Streeter, who wore a flowing beard because he had taken an oath in the 1890's not to shave until populism was victorious; the spokesman for a newer urban progressivism, Fiorello La Guardia, who told the convention he had come "to let you know there are other streets and other attitudes in New York besides Wall Street. I speak for Avenue A and 116th Street, instead of Broad and Wall."

The Progressives named La Follette as their candidate for President and as their Vice-Presidential nominee chose Senator Burton K. Wheeler, the Montana Democrat whose probe had driven Harry Daugherty from the cabinet. The Progressive platform attacked monopoly, urged that Congress be given the power to override the Supreme Court, supported government ownership of railroads and, eventually, of water power resources, backed collective bargaining, and advocated the direct nomination and election of the President.

On June 24 the Democratic party assembled in Madison Square Garden for the famous deadlocked convention. In the midst of a terrible heat wave, the delegates battled for seventeen days before they could agree on a platform and candidates. The year 1924 marked the point in the urbanization of America when an unfortunate equilibrium was struck between the urban Northeast and the rural South and West. Both the urban and rural elements made a bad showing at the convention. Democrats from the South and West emerged as racial bigots who championed the Ku Klux Klan (Texas delegates had to be dissuaded from burning a fiery cross); the New Yorkers appeared to no better advantage as they shouted down Bryan and behaved like Cockney rowdies. So closely was the convention divided that the vote not to mention the Klan by name in the platform was passed 543$\frac{3}{20}$ to 542$\frac{3}{20}$.

The convention divided in the same fashion on choosing a presidential nominee. For nine hot days the delegates deadlocked between New York's Governor Alfred E. Smith and McAdoo, the hero of the South and West. (Will Rogers wrote during the convention: "This thing has got to come to an end. New York invited you people here as guests, not to live.") Smith partisans in the galleries jeered at McAdoo, "Oil! Oil! Oil!" and boasted that there was "No Oil on Al." After 95 ballots, Smith and McAdoo withdrew by agreement; on the 103d ballot, the convention named John W. Davis for President and then chose Charles Bryan for Vice-President. Davis, Solicitor-General under Wilson and ambassador to Great Britain, was a man of ability and character ("the type," noted a political writer sardonically, "that street-railway conductors like to have for a superintendent—that is, 'a mighty fine man' "). As one of the leading corporation lawyers in the country, however, he was a red flag to the Progressive bulls. Moreover, naming William Jennings Bryan's younger brother as the vice-presidential candidate made the ticket look too obviously contrived, not the expression of a popular demand but the work of backroom politicians—Wall Street and Bryan on the same ticket. By the end of the convention, neither nomination was worth a lead nickel. Once again the Democratic party had revealed itself to be "merely an aggregation of local interests" resembling "the old Austrian Empire."

The Republican party pursued the shrewd strategy of ignoring the Democrats. Calvin Coolidge sat out the campaign in the White House, leaving the strenuous barnstorming to the Republican vice-presidential candidate Charles "Hell and Maria" Dawes. Dawes concentrated his fire on La Follette. Although the La Follette program was on the whole moderate, and although La

Follette had flatly spurned Communist support (and was bitterly and unfairly maligned by the Communists), Dawes and the Republicans insinuated that the Senator was a bolshevik agent. The issue in 1924, declared Coolidge, was "whether America will allow itself to be degraded into a communistic or socialistic state or whether it will remain American." Pointing to the Progressive pledge to reform the Supreme Court, and warning that a vote for La Follette might prevent any candidate from winning a majority and might thus throw the election into the House of Representatives, the Republicans argued that the only issue was, in George Harvey's phrase, "Coolidge or Chaos." In this curiously unreal campaign, the Democratic party made less impression on the popular mind than at any other time in its history. Davis could not get the Republicans to notice him, and La Follette could not for long distract the Republican press from the false issue of communism. The Republican campaign was a successful application of Philip Guedalla's dictum, "Any stigma would do to beat a dogma."

The Progressives, although they had a new interest in bread and butter issues, based their 1924 campaign on the old cry of the evil of monopoly. In the postwar years, noted one writer, an attack on the trusts seemed as outdated as the tandem bicycle and "trust-buster" was a term as much lost in the mists of the past as "free-soiler." In attempting to win public attention on the issue of monopoly, La Follette seemed, as Dos Passos later wrote, "an orator haranguing from the capitol of a lost republic." He appeared to be trying to turn back time to the pre-industrial society of the nineteenth century. The theme song of the 1924 campaign, a La Follette leader later

observed, should have been "Tenting Tonight on the Old Camp Ground."

The Progressives waged the 1924 campaign under insurmountable handicaps. They had no state, county, or municipal tickets, for the unions and the farm organizations would not commit themselves to a third party; the Progressive movement of 1924 was not a third party but merely a presidential and vice-presidential ticket. The Progressives were crippled by lack of money; for every dollar Coolidge had in campaign funds, La Follette had four cents. Their appeal to the farmer was blunted by a sharp rise in farm prices. The AF of L, which indorsed La Follette in 1924 and thus broke its tradition of never making an outright indorsement of a Presidential candidate, gave little material aid to the Progressive campaign; some unions, like the Carpenters under Big Bill Hutcheson and the Mine Workers under John L. Lewis, even supported Coolidge.

Calvin Coolidge swept the country with 15 million votes, Davis was second with the unbelievably low total of 8 million, and La Follette trailed with somewhat less than 5 million votes. So great was the Republican margin that Coolidge got more votes than both his opponents put together in all but nine states. Eight years before, the Democrats had been the majority party. In 1924, they had sunk to such relative unimportance that not only were they engulfed by the Republican party but La Follette and the Progressives got four times as many votes as the Democratic ticket in California and twice as many votes as Davis in seventeen states west of the Mississippi. La Follette carried the city of Cleveland, a stronghold of the railway unions, and won 70,000 votes in San

Francisco (Coolidge had 73,000), where Davis polled only 9,800. Yet the Progressives could draw little satisfaction from the election; they had not only helped produce the Coolidge landslide, by splitting the opposition and arousing the fear of "chaos," but La Follette was able to carry only the single state of Wisconsin in the Electoral College.

After the 1924 campaign the movement for a permanent farmer-labor party collapsed. The railway unions pulled out, and only a tiny fragment was left to struggle on for a few more years and then die. (The ideal of a farmer-labor party had always been something of a mirage. An Indiana farmer scolded Coolidge to "get the viewpoint of the broad prairie farmer. Don't be a narrow minded hillbilly from Vermont dominated by selfish money and manufacturing and union labor interests all your life.") Before the war, progressivism had secured its greatest triumphs in an era of prosperity, but in the boom years of the Coolidge era, it got nowhere. When utilities announced high profits, people responded not with a wave of indignation but with a rush to buy utility stocks. In Congress the progressive bloc continued to score Pyrrhic victories, but even there the progressives were dispirited and discouraged.

Baffled progressives looked back nostalgically to their era of influence, unable to puzzle out the reasons for their loss of prestige or to understand why so many of their former leaders had abandoned politics altogether. In a symposium in 1926, the economist Stuart Chase wrote of the prewar era:

Them was the days! When the muckrakers were best sellers, when trust busters were swinging their lariats over every state capitol, when "priviledge" shook in its shoes, when God was behind the initiative, the referendum and the recall—and the devil shrieked when he saw the short ballot, when the Masses was at the height of its glory, and Utopia was just around the corner....

Now look at the damned thing. You could put the avowed Socialists into a roomy new house, Mr. Coolidge is compared favorably to Lincoln, the short ballot is as defunct as Mah Jong, Mr. Eastman writes triolets in France, Mr. Steffens has bought him a castle in Italy, and Mr. Howe digs turnips in Nantucket.

Shall we lay a wreath on the Uplift Movement in America? I suppose we might as well.

The 1920's marked a time of transition within progressivism from the old-style evangelical reformism, under leaders like La Follette and Bryan, to a new style urban progressivism, which would call itself liberalism. Liberalism would be less interested in the moral reformation of man and more in using the power of the federal government to provide specific economic and social benefits. Unlike progressivism, which drew its strength from the old-stock middle class of the small towns and the cities, with not a little support from rural areas, liberalism would be centered in the urban masses, often the "new" immigrant workers of the great cities.

Progressivism was frustrated in the 1920's because, even when it held the balance of power in Congress, it had no program to present; it was reduced to guerilla sniping at the conservatives, who knew what they wanted. Because the progressives had no program that required large-scale government spending, they eventually were forced, in the face of a bulging Treasury surplus, to agree to Mellon's tax cuts. Yet, although the progressives had few accomplishments in the 1920's, they were laying the basis for a change in attitude without which the

New Deal would not have been possible. McNary-Haugenism committed the farmer to using the taxing power to subsidize agriculture; the Muscle Shoals fight paved the way for the public power projects of the 1930's; and the Railway Labor Act of 1926 was an important forerunner of the Wagner Act of 1935. At the same time, a corps of economists—men like Wesley Mitchell, Walton Hamilton, Paul Douglas, and Rexford Tugwell—were hammering out the theoretical foundations of the New Deal.

The new progressivism was already beginning to make its way in the 1920's, notably in the career of Fiorello La Guardia, who as congressman from New York City's East Harlem delighted in taunting the Old Guard leadership of the Republican party. La Guardia said to a reporter in 1922, "I stand for the Republicanism of Abraham Lincoln; and let me tell you that the average Republican leader east of the Mississippi doesn't know anything more about Abraham Lincoln than Henry Ford knows about the Talmud." La Guardia, who was a spokesman for the urban immigrant and thus was opposed to nativism and basically interested in cost-of-living issues, would link the older Progressives with the New Dealers; in the 1920's he was one of the few exceptions to the conservatism of the great cities. The new-style liberalism had not yet gained any considerable strength, while the old-style progressivism was dying out. Some men, of course, such as George Norris and even La Follette and Bryan to some extent, successfully combined elements of both. But in 1925 La Follette and Bryan died, and in 1926 Debs also passed away. ("It is hard," said Senator Borah after hearing of La Follette's death, "to say the right thing about Bob La Follette. You know he lived 150 years.") Until the urban progressives gained greater strength and until they found a national leader who could heal the breach between the two traditions, the progressives had little hope of winning national power.

ARTHUR S. LINK (1920–   ), Woodrow Wilson's most
thorough and recent biographer, has a higher opinion
of Progressivism than does Leuchtenburg. In the
following article he differs with the latter historian over
both the causes ending the Progressive era and the
continuing vitality of the Progressive impulse in the
1920s. Their disagreement is not only a matter of
evidence; it also derives from the meaning one attaches
to modern liberalism. Born in Virginia and educated
at the University of North Carolina, Professor Link
teaches at Princeton and is the author of a standard
textbook of twentieth-century American history.*

Not So Tired

If the day has not yet arrived when we
can make a definite synthesis of political
developments between the Armistice and
the Great Depression, it is surely high
time for historians to begin to clear away
the accumulated heap of mistaken and
half-mistaken hypotheses about this important transitional period. Writing
often without fear or much research
(to paraphrase Carl Becker's remark),
we recent American historians have gone
on indefatigably to perpetuate hypotheses that either reflected the disillusionment and despair of contemporaries, or
once served their purpose in exposing

the alleged hiatus in the great con-
tinuum of twentieth-century reform.

Stated briefly, the following are what
might be called the governing hypotheses of the period under discussion: The
1920's were a period made almost unique
by an extraordinary reaction against
idealism and reform. They were a time
when the political representatives of big
business and Wall Street executed a relentless and successful campaign in state
and nation to subvert the regulatory
structure that had been built at the cost
of so much toil and sweat since the
1870's, and to restore a Hanna-like reign

* Arthur S. Link, "What Happened to the Progressive Movement in the 1920's?"
American Historical Review, LXIV (July 1959), 833–851. Reprinted by permission of the
author and the American Historical Association.

of special privilege to benefit business, industry, and finance. The surging tides of nationalism and mass hatreds generated by World War I continued to engulf the land and were manifested, among other things, in fear of communism, suppression of civil liberties, revival of nativism and anti-Semitism most crudely exemplified by the Ku Klux Klan, and in the triumph of racism and prejudice in immigration legislation. The 1920's were an era when great traditions and ideals were repudiated or forgotten, when the American people, propelled by a crass materialism in their scramble for wealth, uttered a curse on twenty-five years of reform endeavor. As a result, progressives were stunned and everywhere in retreat along the entire political front, their forces disorganized and leaderless, their movement shattered, their dreams of a new America turned into agonizing nightmares.

To be sure, the total picture that emerges from these generalizations is overdrawn. Yet it seems fair to say that leading historians have advanced each of these generalizations, that the total picture is the one that most of us younger historians saw during the years of our training, and that these hypotheses to a greater or lesser degree still control the way in which we write and teach about the 1920's, as a reading of textbooks and general works will quickly show.

This paper has not been written, however, to quarrel with anyone or to make an indictment. Its purposes are, first, to attempt to determine the degree to which the governing hypotheses, as stated, are adequate or inadequate to explain the political phenomena of the period, and, second to discover whether any new and sounder hypotheses might be suggested. Such an effort, of course, must be tentative and above all imper-

fect in view of the absence of sufficient foundations for a synthesis.

Happily, however, we do not have to proceed entirely in the dark. Historians young and old, but mostly young, have already discovered that the period of the 1920's is the exciting new frontier of American historical research and that its opportunities are almost limitless in view of the mass of manuscript materials that are becoming available. Thus we have (the following examples are mentioned only at random) excellent recent studies of agrarian discontent and farm movements by Theodore Saloutos, John D. Hicks, Gilbert C. Fite, Robert L. Morlan, and James H. Shideler; of nativism and problems of immigration and assimilation by John Higham, Oscar Handlin, Robert A. Devine, and Edmund D. Cronon; of intellectual currents, the social gospel, and religious controversies by Henry F. May, Paul A. Carter, Robert M. Miller, and Norman F. Furniss; of left-wing politics and labor developments by Theodore Draper, David A. Shannon, Daniel Bell, Paul M. Angle, and Matthew Josephson; of the campaign of 1928 by Edmund A. Moore; and of political and judicial leaders by Alpheus T. Mason, Frank Freidel, Arthur M. Schlesinger, Jr., Merlo J. Pusey, and Joel F. Paschal.[1] Moreover, we can look forward to the early publication of studies that will be equally illuminating for the period, like

1 Theodore Saloutos and John D. Hicks, *Agrarian Discontent in the Middle West, 1900–1939* (Madison, Wis., 1951); Gilbert C. Fite, *Peter Norbeck: Prairie Statesman* (Columbia, Mo., 1948), and *George N. Peek and the Fight for Farm Parity* (Norman, Okla., 1954); Robert L. Morlan, *Political Prairie Fire: The Nonpartisan League, 1915–1922* (Minneapolis, Minn., 1955); James H. Shideler, *Farm Crisis, 1919–1923* (Berkeley, Calif., 1957); John Higham, *Strangers in the Land: Patterns of American Nativism, 1860–1925* (New Brunswick, N. J., 1955); Oscar Handlin, *The American People in the Twentieth*

the biographies of George W. Norris, Thomas J. Walsh, and Albert B. Fall now being prepared by Richard Lowitt, Leonard Bates, and David Stratton, respectively, and the recently completed study of the campaign and election of 1920 by Wesley M. Bagby.[2]

Obviously, we are not only at a point in the progress of our research into the political history of the 1920's when we

Century (Cambridge, Mass., 1954); Robert A. Devine, *American Immigration Policy, 1924–1952* (New Haven, Conn., 1957); Edmund D. Cronon, *Black Moses: The Story of Marcus Garvey and the Universal Negro Improvement Association* (Madison, Wis., 1955); Henry F. May, "Shifting Perspectives on the 1920's," *Mississippi Valley Historical Review,* XLIII (Dec., 1956), 405–27; Paul A. Carter, *The Decline and Revival of the Social Gospel* (Ithaca, N. Y., 1956); Robert M. Miller, "An Inquiry into the Social Attitudes of American Protestantism, 1919–1939," doctoral dissertation, Northwestern University, 1955; Norman F. Furniss, *The Fundamentalist Controversy, 1918–1931* (New Haven, Conn., 1954); Theodore Draper, *The Roots of American Communism* (New York, 1957); David A. Shannon, *The Socialist Party of America: A History* (New York, 1955); Daniel Bell, "The Background and Development of Marxian Socialism in the United States," *Socialism and American Life,* ed. Donald D. Egbert and Stow Persons (2 vols., Princeton, N. J., 1952), I, 215–405; Paul M. Angle, *Bloody Williamson* (New York, 1952); Matthew Josephson, *Sidney Hillman: Statesman of American Labor* (New York, 1952); Edmund A. Moore, *A Catholic Runs for President: The Campaign of 1928* (New York, 1956); Alpheus Thomas Mason, *Brandeis: A Free Man's Life* (New York, 1946), and *Harlan Fiske Stone: Pillar of the Law* (New York, 1956); Frank Freidel, *Franklin D. Roosevelt: The Ordeal* (Boston, 1954); Arthur M. Schlesinger, Jr., *The Age of Roosevelt: The Crisis of the Old Order* (Boston, 1957); Merlo J. Pusey, *Charles Evans Hughes* (2 vols., New York, 1951); Joel Francis Paschal, *Mr. Justice Sutherland: A Man against the State* (Princeton, N. J., 1951).

2 Wesley M. Bagby, "Woodrow Wilson and the Great Debacle of 1920," MS in the possession of Professor Bagby; see also his "The 'Smoked-Filled Room' and the Nomination of Warren G. Harding," *Mississippi Valley Historical Review,* XLI (Mar., 1955), 657–74, and "Woodrow Wilson, a Third Term, and the Solemn Referendum," *American Historical Review,* LX (Apr., 1955), 567–75.

can begin to generalize, but we have reached the time when we should attempt to find some consensus, however tentative it must now be, concerning the larger political dimensions and meanings of the period.

In answering the question of what happened to the progressive movement in the 1920's, we should begin by looking briefly at some fundamental facts about the movement before 1918, facts that in large measure predetermined its fate in the 1920's, given the political climate and circumstances that prevailed.

The first of these was the elementary fact that the progressive movement never really existed as a recognizable organization with common goals and a political machinery geared to achieve them. Generally speaking (and for the purposes of this paper), progressivism might be defined as the popular effort, which began convulsively in the 1890's and waxed and waned afterward to our own time, to insure the survival of democracy in the United States by the enlargement of governmental power to control and offset the power of private economic groups over the nation's institutions and life. Actually, of course, from the 1890's on there were many "progressive" movements on many levels seeking sometimes contradictory objectives. Not all, but most of these campaigns were the work of special interest groups or classes seeking greater political status and economic security. This was true from the beginning of the progressive movement in the 1890's; by 1913 it was that movement's most important characteristic.

The second fundamental fact—that the progressive movements were often largely middle class in constituency and orientation—is of course well known, but an important corollary has often been ignored. It was that several of the most important reform movements were inspired, staffed, and led by businessmen with very specific or special-interest objectives in view. Because they hated waste, mismanagement, and high taxes, they, together with their friends in the legal profession, often furnished the leadership of good government campaigns. Because they feared industrial monopoly, abuse of power by railroads, and the growth of financial oligarchy, they were the backbone of the movements that culminated in the adoption of the Hepburn and later acts for railroad regulation, the Federal Reserve Act, and the Federal Trade Commission Act. Among the many consequences of their participation in the progressive movement, two should be mentioned because of their significance for developments in the 1920's: First, the strong identification of businessmen with good government and economic reforms for which the general public also had a lively concern helped preserve the good reputation of the middle-class business community (as opposed to its alleged natural enemies, monopolists, malefactors of great wealth, and railroad barons) and helped to direct the energies of the progressive movement toward the strengthening instead of the shackling of the business community. Second, their activities and influence served to intensify the tensions within the broad reform movement, because they often opposed the demands of farm groups, labor unions, and advocates of social justice.

The third remark to be made about the progressive movement before 1918 is that despite its actual diversity and inner tensions it did seem to have unity; that is, it seemed to share common ideals and objectives. This was true in part because much of the motivation even of the special-interest groups was altruistic (at least they succeeded in convincing themselves that they sought the welfare of society rather than their own interests primarily); in part because political leadership generally succeeded in subordinating inner tensions. It was true, above all, because there were in fact important idealistic elements in the progressive ranks—social gospel leaders, social justice elements, and intellectuals and philosophers—who worked hard at the task of defining and elevating common principles and goals.

Fourth and finally, the substantial progressive achievements before 1918 had been gained, at least on the federal level, only because of the temporary dislocations of the national political structure caused by successive popular uprisings, not because progressives had found or created a viable organization for perpetuating their control. Or, to put the matter another way, before 1918 the various progressive elements had failed to destroy the existing party structure by organizing a national party of their own that could survive. They, or at least many of them, tried in 1912; and it seemed for a time in 1916 that Woodrow Wilson had succeeded in drawing the important progressive groups permanently into the Democratic party. But Wilson's accomplishment did not survive even to the end of the war, and by 1920 traditional partisan loyalties were reasserting themselves with extraordinary vigor.

With this introduction, we can now ask what happened to the progressive movement or movements in the 1920's. Surely no one would contend that after 1916 the political scene did not change significantly, both on the state and national levels. There was the seemingly obvious fact that the Wilsonian coalition had been wrecked by the election of 1920, and that the progressive elements were divided and afterward unable to agree upon a program or to control the national government. There was the even more "obvious" fact that conservative Republican presidents and their cabinets controlled the executive branch throughout the period. There was Congress, as Eric F. Goldman had said, allegedly whopping through pro-corporation legislation, and the Supreme Court interpreting the New Freedom laws in a way that harassed unions and encouraged trusts.[3] There were, to outraged idealists and intellectuals, the more disgusting spectacles of Red hunts, mass arrests and deportations, the survival deep into the 1920's of arrogant nationalism, crusades against the teaching of evolution, the attempted suppression of the right to drink, and myriad other manifestations of what would now be called a repressive reaction.[4]

Like the hypotheses suggested at the beginning, this picture is overdrawn in some particulars. But it is accurate in part, for progressivism was certainly on the downgrade if not in decay after 1918. This is an obvious fact that needs explanation and understanding rather than elaborate proof. We can go a long way toward answering our question if we can explain, at least partially, the extraordinary complex developments that converge to produce the "obvious" result.

[3] Eric F. Goldman, *Rendezvous with Destiny* (New York, 1953), 284. The "allegedly" in this sentence is mine, not Professor Goldman's.

[4] H. C. Peterson and Gilbert C. Fite, *Opponents of War, 1917–1918* (Norman, Okla., 1957); Robert K. Murray, *Red Scare: A Study in National Hysteria, 1919–1920* (Minneapolis, Minn., 1955).

For this explanation we must begin by looking at the several progressive elements and their relation to each other and to the two major parties after 1916. Since national progressivism was never an organized or independent movement (except imperfectly and then only temporarily in 1912), it could succeed only when its constituent elements formed a coalition strong enough to control one of the major parties. This had happened in 1916, when southern and western farmers, organized labor, the social justice elements, and a large part of the independent radicals who had heretofore voted the Socialist ticket coalesced to continue the control of Wilson and the Democratic party.

The important fact about the progressive coalition of 1916, however, was not its strength but its weakness. It was not a new party but a temporary alliance, welded in the heat of the most extraordinary domestic and external events. To be sure, it functioned for the most part successfully during the war, in providing the necessary support for a program of heavy taxation, relatively stringent controls over business and industry, and extensive new benefits to labor. Surviving in a crippled way even in the months following the Armistice, it put across a program that constituted a sizable triumph for the progressive movement—continued heavy taxation, the Transportation Act of 1920, the culmination of the long fight for railroad regulation, a new child labor act, amendments for prohibition and woman suffrage, immigration restriction, and water power and conservation legislation.

Even so, the progressive coalition of 1916 was inherently unstable. Indeed, it was so wracked by inner tensions that it could not survive, and destruction came inexorably, it seemed systematically, from 1917 to 1920. Why was this true?

First, the independent radicals and antiwar agrarians were alienated by the war declaration and the government's suppression of dissent and civil liberties during the war and the Red scare. Organized labor was disaffected by the administration's coercion of the coal miners in 1919, its lukewarm if not hostile attitude during the great strikes of 1919 and 1920, and its failure to support the Plumb Plan for nationalization of the railroads. Isolationists and idealists were outraged by what they thought was the President's betrayal of American traditions or the liberal peace program at Paris. These tensions were strong enough to disrupt the coalition, but a final one would have been fatal even if the others had never existed. This was the alienation of farmers in the Plains and western states produced by the administration's refusal to impose price controls on cotton while it maintained ceilings on the prices of other agricultural commodities,[5] and especially by the administration's failure to do anything decisive to stem the downward plunge of farm prices that began in the summer of 1920.[6] Under the impact of all these stresses, the Wilsonian coalition gradually disintegrated from

5 On this point, see Seward W. Livermore, "The Sectional Issue in the 1918 Congressional Elections," *Mississippi Valley Historical Review*, XXXV (June, 1948), 29–60.

6 Arthur S. Link, "The Federal Reserve Policy and the Agricultural Depression of 1920–1921," *Agricultural History*, XX (July, 1946), 166–75; and Herbert F. Margulies, "The Election of 1920 in Wisconsin: The Return to 'Normalcy' Reappraised," *Wisconsin Magazine of History*, XXXVIII (Autumn, 1954), 15–22.

1917 to 1920 and disappeared entirely during the campaign of 1920.

The progressive coalition was thus destroyed, but the components of a potential movement remained. As we will see, these elements were neither inactive nor entirely unsuccessful in the 1920's. But they obviously failed to find common principles and a program, much less to unite effectively for political action on a national scale. I suggest that this was true, in part at least, for the following reasons:

First, the progressive elements could never create or gain control of a political organization capable of carrying them into national office. The Republican party was patently an impossible instrument because control of the GOP was too much in the hands of the eastern and midwestern industrial, oil, and financial interests, as it had been since about 1910. There was always the hope of a third party. Several progressive groups—insurgent midwestern Republicans, the railroad brotherhoods, a segment of the AF of L, and the moderate Socialists under Robert M. La Follette—tried to realize this goal in 1924, only to discover that third party movements in the United States are doomed to failure except in periods of enormous national turmoil, and that the 1920's were not such a time. Thus the Democratic party remained the only vehicle that conceivably could have been used by a new progressive coalition. But that party was simply not capable of such service in the 1920's. It was so torn by conflicts between its eastern, big city wing and its southern and western rural majority that it literally ceased to be a national party. It remained strong in its sectional and metropolitan components, but it was so divided that it barely succeeded in nominating a presidential candidate at all in 1924 and nominated one in 1928 only at the cost of temporary disruption.[7]

Progressivism declined in the 1920's, in the second place, because, as has been suggested, the tensions that had wrecked the coalition of 1916 not only persisted but actually grew in number and intensity. The two most numerous progressive elements, the southern and western farmers, strongly supported the Eighteenth Amendment, were heavily tinged with nativism and therefore supported immigration restriction, were either members of, friendly to, or politically afraid of the Ku Klux Klan, and demanded as the principal plank in their platform legislation to guarantee them a larger share of the national income. On all these points and issues the lower and lower middle classes in the large cities stood in direct and often violent opposition to their potential allies in the rural areas. Moreover, the liaison between the farm groups and organized labor, which had been productive of much significant legislation during the Wilson period, virtually ceased to exist in the 1920's. There were many reasons for this development, and I mention only one—the fact that the preeminent spokesmen of farmers in the 1920's, the new Farm Bureau Federation, represented the larger commercial farmers who (in contrast to the members of the leading farm organization in Wilson's day, the National Farmers' Union) were often employers themselves and felt no identification with the rank and file of labor.

[7] For a highly partisan account of these events see Karl Schriftgiesser, *This Was Normalcy* (Boston, 1948). More balanced are the already cited Freidel, *Franklin D. Roosevelt: The Ordeal,* and Schlesinger, *The Age of Roosevelt: The Crisis of the Old Order.*

It was little wonder, therefore (and this is a third reason for the weakness of progressivism in the 1920's), that the tension-ridden progressive groups were never able to agree upon a program that, like the Democratic platform of 1916, could provide the basis for a revived coalition. So long as progressive groups fought one another more fiercely than they fought their natural opponents, such agreement was impossible; and so long as common goals were impossible to achieve, a national progressive movement could not take effective form. Nothing illustrates this better than the failure of the Democratic conventions of 1924 and 1928 to adopt platforms that could rally and unite the discontented elements. One result, among others, was that southern farmers voted as Democrats and western farmers as Republicans. And, as Professor Frank Freidel once commented to the author, much of the failure of progressivism in the 1920's can be explained by this elementary fact.

A deeper reason for the failure of progressives to unite ideologically in the 1920's was what might be called a substantial paralysis of the progressive mind. This was partly the result of the repudiation of progressive ideals by many intellectuals and the defection from the progressive movement of the urban middle classes and professional groups, as will be demonstrated. It was the result, even more importantly, of the fact that progressivism as an organized body of political thought found itself at a crossroads in the 1920's, like progressivism today, and did not know which way to turn. The major objectives of the progressive movement of the prewar years had in fact been largely achieved by 1920. In what direction should progressivism now move? Should it remain in the channels already deeply cut by its own traditions, and, while giving sincere allegiance to the ideal of democratic capitalism, work for more comprehensive programs of business regulation and assistance to disadvantaged classes like farmers and submerged industrial workers? Should it abandon these traditions and, like most similar European movements, take the road toward a moderate socialism with a predominantly labor orientation? Should it attempt merely to revive the goals of more democracy through changes in the political machinery? Or should it become mainly an agrarian movement with purely agrarian goals?

These were real dilemmas, not academic ones, and one can see numerous examples of how they confused and almost paralyzed progressives in the 1920's. The platform of La Follette's Progressive party of 1924 offers one revealing illustration. It embodied much that was old and meaningless by this time (the direct election of the president and a national referendum before the adoption of a war resolution, for example) and little that had any real significance for the future.[8] And yet it was the best that a vigorous and idealistic movement could offer. A second example was the plight of the agrarians and insurgents in Congress who fought so hard all through the 1920's against Andrew Mellon's proposals to abolish the inheritance tax and to make drastic reductions in the taxes on large incomes. In view of the rapid reduction of the federal debt,

the progressives were hard pressed to justify the continuation of nearly confiscatory tax levels, simply because few of them realized the wide social and economic uses to which the income tax could be put. Lacking any programs for the redistribution of the national income (except to farmers), they were plagued and overwhelmed by the surpluses in the federal Treasury until, for want of any good arguments, they finally gave Secretary Andrew Mellon the legislation he had been demanding.[9] A third and final example of this virtual paralysis of the progressive mind was perhaps the most revealing of all. It was the attempt that Woodrow Wilson, Louis D. Brandeis, and other Democratic leaders made from 1921 to 1924 to draft a new charter for progressivism. Except for its inevitable proposals for an idealistic world leadership, the document that emerged from this interchange included little or nothing that would have sounded new to a western progressive in 1912.

A fourth reason for the disintegration and decline of the progressive movement in the 1920's was the lack of any effective leadership. Given the political temper and circumstances of the 1920's, it is possible that such leadership could not have operated successfully in any event. Perhaps the various progressive elements were so mutually hostile and so self-centered in interests and objectives that even a Theodore Roosevelt or a Woodrow Wilson, had they been at the zenith of their powers in the 1920's, could not have drawn them together in a common front. We will never know what a strong national leader might have done because by a trick of fate no such leader emerged before Franklin D. Roosevelt.

[8] For a different picture see Belle C. La Follette and Fola La Follette, *Robert M. La Follette* (2 vols., New York, 1953); and Russel B. Nye, *Midwestern Progressive Politics, 1870–1950* (East Lansing, Mich., 1951). Both works contribute to an understanding of progressive politics in the 1920's.

[9] Here indebtedness is acknowledged to Sidney Ratner, *American Taxation: Its History as a Social Force in Democracy* (New York, 1942).

Four factors, then, contributed to the failure of the progressive components to unite successfully after 1918 and, as things turned out, before 1932: the lack of a suitable political vehicle, the severity of the tensions that kept progressives apart, the failure of progressives to agree upon a common program, and the absence of a national leadership, without which a united movement could never be created and sustained. These were all weaknesses that stemmed to a large degree from the instability and failures of the progressive movement itself.

There were, besides, a number of what might be called external causes for the movement's decline. In considering them one must begin with what was seemingly the most important—the alleged fact that the 1920's were a very unpropitious time for any new progressive revolt because of the ever-increasing level of economic prosperity, the materialism, and the general contentment of the decade 1919 to 1929. Part of this generalization is valid when applied to specific elements in the population. For example, the rapid rise in the real wages of industrial employment and the spread of so-called welfare practices among management, certainly did much to weaken and avert the further spread of organized labor, and thus to debilitate one of the important progressive components. But to say that it was prosperity per se that created a climate unfriendly to progressive ideals would be inaccurate. There was little prosperity and much depression during the 1920's for the single largest economic group, the farmers, as well as for numerous other groups. Progressivism, moreover, can flourish as much during periods of prosperity as during periods of discontent, as the history of the development of the progressive movement from 1901 to 1917 and of its triumph from 1945 to 1956 prove.

Vastly more important among the external factors in the decline of progressivism was the widespread, almost wholesale, defection from its ranks of the middle classes—the middling businessmen, bankers, and manufacturers, and the professional people closely associated with them in ideals and habits—in American cities large and small. For an understanding of this phenomenon no simple explanations like "prosperity" or the "temper of the times" will suffice, although they give some insight. The important fact was that these groups found a new economic and social status as a consequence of the flowering of American enterprise under the impact of the technological, financial, and other revolutions of the 1920's. If, as Professor Richard Hofstadter had claimed,[10] the urban middle classes were progressive (that is, they demanded governmental relief from various anxieties) in the early 1900's because they resented their loss of social prestige to the *nouveaux riches* and feared being ground under by monopolists in industry, banking, and labor—if this is true, then the urban middle classes were not progressive in the 1920's for inverse reasons. Their temper was dynamic, expansive, and supremely confident. They knew that they were building a new America, a business civilization based not upon monopoly and restriction but upon a whole new set of business values—mass production and consumption, short hours and high wages, full employment, welfare capitalism. And what was more important, virtually the entire country (at least the journalists, writers in popular magazines,

[10] Richard Hofstadter, *The Age of Reform: From Bryan to F.D.R.* (New York, 1955), 131 ff.

and many preachers and professors) acknowledged that the nation's destiny was in good hands. It was little wonder, therefore, that the whole complex of groups constituting the urban middle classes, whether in New York, Zenith, or Middletown, had little interest in rebellion or even in mild reform proposals that seemed to imperil their leadership and control.

Other important factors, of course, contributed to the contentment of the urban middle classes. The professionalization of business and the full-blown emergence of a large managerial class had a profound impact upon social and political ideals. The acceleration of mass advertising played its role, as did also the beginning disintegration of the great cities with the spread of middle- and upper-middle-class suburbs, a factor that diffused the remaining reform energies among the urban leaders.

A second external factor in the decline of the progressive movement after 1918 was the desertion from its ranks of a good part of the intellectual leadership of the country. Indeed, more than simple desertion was involved here; it was often a matter of a cynical repudiation of the ideals from which progressivism derived its strength. I do not mean to imply too much by this generalization. I know that what has been called intellectual progressivism not only survived in the 1920's but actually flourished in many fields.[11] I know that the intellectual foundations of our present quasi-welfare state were either being laid or reinforced during the decade. Even so, one cannot evade the

conclusion that the intellectual-political climate of the 1920's was vastly different from the one that had prevailed in the preceding two decades.

During the years of the great progressive revolt, intellectuals—novelists, journalists, political thinkers, social scientists, historians, and the like—had made a deeply personal commitment to the cause of democracy, first in domestic and then in foreign affairs. Their leadership in and impact on many phases of the progressive movement had been profound. By contrast, in the 1920's a large body of this intellectual phalanx turned against the very ideals they had once deified. One could cite, for example, the reaction of the idealists against the Versailles settlement; the disenchantment of the intellectuals with the extension of government authority when it could be used to justify the Eighteenth Amendment or the suppression of free speech; or the inevitable loss of faith in the "people" when en masse they hounded so-called radicals, joined Bryan's crusade against evolution, or regaled themselves as Knights of the Ku Klux Klan. Whatever the cause, many alienated intellectuals simply withdrew or repudiated any identification with the groups they had once helped to lead. The result was not fatal to progressivism, but it was serious. The spark plugs had been removed from the engine of reform.

The progressive movement, then, unquestionably declined, but was it defunct in the 1920's? Much, of course, depends upon the definition of terms. If we accept the usual definition for "defunct" as "dead" or "ceasing to have any life or strength," we must recognize that the progressive movement was certainly not defunct in the 1920's; that on the contrary at least important parts of it were

---

11 *Ibid.*, 5, 131, 135 ff. For a recent excellent survey, previously cited, see Henry F. May, "Shifting Perspectives on the 1920's." Schlesinger's previously cited *Age of Roosevelt* sheds much new light on the economic thought of the 1920's.

very much alive; and that it is just as important to know how and why progressivism survived as it is to know how and why it declined.

To state the matter briefly, progressivism survived in the 1920's because several important elements of the movement remained either in full vigor or in only slightly diminished strength. These were the farmers, after 1918 better organized and more powerful than during the high tide of the progressive revolt; the politically conscious elements among organized labor, particularly the railroad brotherhoods, who wielded a power all out of proportion to their numbers; the Democratic organizations in the large cities, usually vitally concerned with the welfare of the so-called lower classes; a remnant of independent radicals, social workers, and social gospel writers and preachers; and finally, an emerging new vocal element, the champions of public power and regional developments.

Although they never united effectively enough to capture a major party and the national government before 1932, these progressive elements controlled Congress from 1921 to about 1927 and continued to exercise a near control during the period of their greatest weakness in the legislative branch, from 1927 to about 1930.

Indeed, the single most powerful and consistently successful group in Congress during the entire decade from 1919 to 1929 were the spokesmen of the farmers. Spurred by an unrest in the country areas more intense than at any time since the 1890's,[12] in 1920 and 1921 southern Democrats and midwestern and western

insurgents, nominally Republican, joined forces in an alliance called the Farm Bloc. By maintaining a common front from 1921 to 1924 they succeeded in enacting the most advanced agricultural legislation to that date, legislation that completed the program begun under Wilsonian auspices. It included measures for high tariffs on agricultural products, thoroughgoing federal regulation of stockyards, packing houses, and grain exchanges, the exemption of agricultural cooperatives from the application of the antitrust laws, stimulation of the export of agricultural commodities, and the establishment of an entirely new federal system of intermediate rural credit.

When prosperity failed to return to the countryside, rural leaders in Congress espoused a new and bolder plan for relief—the proposal made by George N. Peek and Hugh S. Johnson in 1922 to use the federal power to obtain "fair exchange" or "parity" prices for farm products. Embodied in the McNary-Haugen bill in 1924, this measure was approved by Congress in 1927 and 1928, only to encounter vetoes by President Calvin Coolidge.

In spite of its momentary failure, the McNary-Haugen bill had a momentous significance for the American progressive movement. Its wholesale espousal by the great mass of farm leaders and spokesmen meant that the politically most powerful class in the country had come full scale to the conviction that the taxing power should be used directly and specifically for the purpose of underwriting (some persons called it subsidizing) agriculture. It was a milestone in the development of a comprehensive political doctrine that it was government's duty to protect the economic security of all classes and particularly depressed

---

[12] It derived from the fact that farm prices plummeted in 1920 and 1921, and remained so low that farmers, generally speaking, operated at a net capital loss throughout the balance of the decade.

ones. McNary-Haugenism can be seen in its proper perspective if it is remembered that it would have been considered almost absurd in the Wilson period, that it was regarded as radical by nonfarm elements in the 1920's, and that it, or at any rate its fundamental objective, was incorporated almost as a matter of course into basic federal policy in the 1930's.

A second significant manifestation of the survival of progressivism in the 1920's came during the long controversy over public ownership or regulation of the burgeoning electric power industry. In this, as in most of the conflicts that eventually culminated on Capitol Hill, the agrarian element constituted the core of progressive strength. At the same time a sizable and well-organized independent movement developed that emanated from urban centers and was vigorous on the municipal and state levels. Throughout the decade this relatively new progressive group fought with mounting success to expose the propaganda of the private utilities, to strengthen state and federal regulatory agencies, and to win municipal ownership for distributive facilities. Like the advocates of railroad regulation in an earlier period, these proponents of regulation or ownership of a great new natural monopoly failed almost as much as they had succeeded in the 1920's. But their activities and exposures (the Federal Trade Commission's devastating investigation of the electric power industry in the late 1920's and early 1930's was the prime example) laid secure foundations for movements that the 1930's would reach various culminations.

Even more significant for the future of American progressivism was the emergence in the 1920's of a new objective, that of committing the federal government to plans for large hydroelectric

projects in the Tennessee Valley, the Columbia River watershed, the Southwest, and the St. Lawrence Valley for the purpose, some progressives said, of establishing "yardsticks" for rates, or for the further purpose, as other progressives declared, of beginning a movement for the eventual nationalization of the entire electric power industry. The development of this movement in its emerging stages affords a good case study in the natural history of American progressivism. It began when the Harding and Coolidge administrations attempted to dispose of the government's hydroelectric and nitrate facilities at Muscle Shoals, Alabama, to private interests. In the first stage of the controversy, the progressive objective was merely federal operation of these facilities for the production of cheap fertilizer—a reflection of its exclusive special-interest orientation. Then, as new groups joined the fight to save Muscle Shoals, the objective of public production of cheap electric power came to the fore. Finally, by the end of the 1920's, the objective of a multipurpose regional development in the Tennessee Valley and in other areas as well had taken firm shape.

In addition, by 1928 the agrarians in Congress led by Senator George W. Norris had found enough allies in the two houses and enough support in the country at large to adopt a bill for limited federal development of the Tennessee Valley. Thwarted by President Coolidge's pocket veto, the progressives tried again in 1931, only to meet a second rebuff at the hands of President Herbert Hoover.

All this might be regarded as another milestone in the maturing of American progressivism. It signified a deviation from the older traditions of mere regulation, as President Hoover had said in his veto of the second Muscle Shoals bill, and the triumph of new concepts of direct federal leadership in large-scale development of resources. If progressives had not won their goal by the end of the 1920's, they had at least succeeded in writing what would become perhaps the most important plank in their program for the future.

The maturing of an advanced farm program and the formulation of plans for public power and regional developments may be termed the two most significant progressive achievements on the national level in the 1920's. Others merit only brief consideration. One was the final winning of the old progressive goal of immigration restriction through limited and selective admission. The fact that this movement was motivated in part by racism, nativism, and anti-Semitism (with which, incidentally, a great many if not a majority of progressives were imbued in the 1920's) should not blind us to the fact that it was also progressive. It sought to substitute a so-called scientific and a planned policy for a policy of laissez faire. Its purpose was admittedly to disturb the free operation of the international labor market. Organized labor and social workers had long supported it against the opposition of large employers. And there was prohibition, the most ambitious and revealing progressive experiment of the twentieth century. Even the contemned anti-evolution crusade of Bryan and the fundamentalists and the surging drives for conformity of thought and action in other fields should be mentioned. All these movements stemmed from the conviction that organized public power could and should be used purposefully to achieve fundamental social and so-called moral change. The fact that they were potentially or actively repressive does not mean that they were not progressive. On the contrary, they superbly illustrated the repressive tendencies that inhered in progressivism precisely because it was grounded so much upon majoritarian principles.

Three other developments on the national level that have often been cited as evidences of the failure of progressivism in the 1920's appear in a somewhat different light at second glance. The first was the reversal of the tariff-for-revenue-only tendencies of the Underwood Act with the enactment of the Emergency Tariff Act of 1921 and the Fordney-McCumber Act of 1922. Actually, the adoption of these measures signified, on the whole, not a repudiation but a revival of progressive principles in the realm of federal fiscal policy. A revenue tariff had never been an authentic progressive objective. Indeed, at least by 1913, many progressives, except for some southern agrarians, had concluded that it was retrogressive and had agreed that the tariff laws should be used deliberately to achieve certain national objectives—for example, the crippling of noncompetitive big business by the free admission of articles manufactured by so-called trusts, or benefits to farmers by the free entry of farm implements. Wilson himself had been at least partially converted to these principles by 1916, as his insistence upon the creation of the Federal Tariff Commission and his promise of protection to the domestic chemical industry revealed. As for the tariff legislation of the early 1920's, its only important changes were increased protection for aluminum, chemical products, and agricultural commodities. It left the Underwood rates on the great mass of raw materials and manufactured goods largely undisturbed. It may have been economically short-sighted and a bad example for the rest of the world, but for the most part it was progressive in principle and was the handiwork of the progressive coalition in Congress.

Another development that has often been misunderstood in its relation to the progressive movement was the policies of consistent support that the Harding and Coolidge administrations adopted for business enterprise, particularly the policy of the Federal Trade Commission in encouraging the formation of trade associations and the diminution of certain traditional competitive practices. The significance of all this can easily be overrated. Such policies as these two administrations executed had substantial justification in progressive theory and in precedents clearly established by the Wilson administration.

A third challenge to usual interpretations concerns implications to be drawn from the election of Harding and Coolidge in 1920 and 1924. These elections seem to indicate the triumph of reaction among the mass of American voters. Yet one could argue that both Harding and Coolidge were political accidents, the beneficiaries of grave defects in the American political and constitutional systems. The rank and file of Republican voters demonstrated during the preconvention campaign that they wanted vigorous leadership and a moderately progressive candidate in 1920. They got Harding instead, not because they wanted him, but because unusual circumstances permitted a small clique to thwart the will of the majority.[13] They

took Coolidge as their candidate in 1924 simply because Harding died in the middle of his term and there seemed to be no alternative to nominating the man who had succeeded him in the White House. Further, an analysis of the election returns in 1920 and 1924 will show that the really decisive factor in the victories of Harding and Coolidge was the fragmentation of the progressive movement and the fact that an opposition strong enough to rally and unite the progressive majority simply did not exist.

There remains, finally, a vast area of progressive activity about which we yet know very little. One could mention the continuation of old reform movements and the development of new ones in the cities and states during the years following the Armistice: For example, the steady spread of the city manager form of government, the beginning of zoning and planning movements, and the efforts of the great cities to keep abreast of the transportation revolution then in full swing. Throughout the country the educational and welfare activities of the cities and states steadily increased. Factory legislation matured, while social insurance had its experimental beginnings. Whether such reform impulses were generally weak or strong, one cannot say; but what we do know about developments in cities like Cincinnati and states like New York, Wisconsin, and Louisiana[14] justifies a challenge to the assumption that municipal and state reform energies were dead after 1918 and, incidentally, a plea to young scholars to plow this unworked field of recent American history.

Let us, then, suggest a tentative syn-

[13] Much that is new on the Republican preconvention campaign and convention of 1920 may be found in William T. Hutchinson, *Lowden of Illinois: The Life of Frank O. Lowden* (2 vols., Chicago, 1957).

[14] See, e.g., Allan P. Sindler, *Huey Long's Louisiana: State Politics, 1920–1952* (Baltimore, Md., 1956).

thesis as an explanation of what happened to the progressive movement after 1918:

First, the national progressive movement, which had found its most effective embodiment in the coalition of forces that reelected Woodrow Wilson in 1916, was shattered by certain policies that the administration pursued from 1917 to 1920, and by some developments over which the administration had no or only slight control. The collapse that occurred in 1920 was not inevitable and cannot be explained by merely saying that "the war killed the progressive movement."

Second, large and aggressive components of a potential new progressive coalition remained after 1920. These elements never succeeded in uniting effectively before the end of the decade, not because they did not exist, but because they were divided by conflicts among themselves. National leadership, which in any event did not emerge in the 1920's, perhaps could not have succeeded in subduing these tensions and in creating a new common front.

Third, as a result of the foregoing, progressivism as an organized national force suffered a serious decline in the 1920's. This decline was heightened by the defection of large elements among the urban middle classes and the intellectuals, a desertion induced by technological, economic, and demographic changes, and by the outcropping of certain repressive tendencies in progressivism after 1917.

Fourth, in spite of reversals and failures, important components of the national progressive movement survived in considerable vigor and succeeded to a varying degree, not merely in keeping the movement alive, but even in broadening its horizons. This was true particularly of the farm groups and of the coalition concerned with public regulation or ownership of electric power resources. These two groups laid the groundwork in the 1920's for significant new programs in the 1930's and beyond.

Fifth, various progressive coalitions controlled Congress for the greater part of the 1920's and were always a serious threat to the conservative administrations that controlled the executive branch. Because this was true, most of the legislation adopted by Congress during this period, including many measures that historians have inaccurately called reactionary, was progressive in character.

Sixth, the progressive movement in the cities and states was far from dead in the 1920's, although we do not have sufficient evidence to justify any generalizations about the degree of its vigor.

If this tentative and imperfect synthesis has any value, perhaps it is high time that we discard the sweeping generalizations, false hypotheses, and clichés that we have so often used in explaining and characterizing political developments from 1918 to 1929. Perhaps we should try to see these developments for what they were—the normal and ordinary political behavior of groups and classes caught up in a swirl of social and economic change. When we do this we will no longer ask whether the progressive movement was defunct in the 1920's. We will ask only what happened to it and why.

Suggestions for Further Reading

The best starting point for the subject is George E. Mowry's succinct and lucid pamphlet, "The Progressive Movement, 1900–1920: Recent Ideas and New Literature" (Washington, D.C., 1958). For the relationship of Progressivism to Populism and the New Deal—and the literature about it—see Arthur Mann, "The Progressive Tradition," in John Higham, ed., *The Reconstruction of American History* (New York, 1962), 157–179.

John D. Hicks, *The Populist Revolt* (Minneapolis, 1931), is still indispensable for that subject. Two books stressing the influence of Populism on later reform movements are Russell B. Nye, *Midwestern Progressive Politics: A Historical Study of Its Origins and Development, 1870–1950* (East Lansing, Mich., 1951), and Theodore Saloutos and John D. Hicks, *Agricultural Discontent in the Middle West, 1900–1939* (Madison, Wis., 1951). C. Vann Woodward is excellent on Southern Populism and Progressivism in *The Origins of the New South, 1877–1913* (Baton Rouge, 1951). Students who like the biographical approach will profit from C. Vann Woodward, *Tom Watson, Agrarian Rebel* (New York, 1938), and Francis B. Simkins, *Pitchfork Ben Tillman, South Carolinian* (Baton Rouge, 1944).

The most influential criticism of Populism is contained in Richard Hofstadter's *The Age of Reform: From Bryan to F.D.R.* (New York, 1955). See also Albert D. Kirwin, *Revolt of the Rednecks: Mississippi Politics, 1876–1925* (Lexington, Ky., 1951); Daniel Bell, ed., *The New American Right* (New York, 1955); and Victor C. Ferkiss, "Populist Influences on American Fascism," *Western Political Quarterly*, X (June 1957), 350–373.

Norman Pollack has written two rebuttals in defense of the Populist crusade: "Hofstadter on Populism: A Critique of 'The Age of Reform,'" *Journal of Southern History*, XXVI (November 1960), 478–500, and "The Myth of Populist Anti-Semitism," *American Historical Review* LXVIII (October 1962), 76–80. There is a further defense of Populism in C. Vann Woodward, "The Populist Heritage and the Intellectual," *American Scholar*, XXIX (Winter 1959–1960), 55–72. For Hicks' justification of his own work, see his "Reform Cycles in Recent American History," *Idaho Yesterdays*, VI (Summer 1962), 11–15, 18–21.

The role of urban reformers in the pre-Progressive era is at the center of Sidney Fine's exhaustive *Laissez Faire and the General-Welfare State: A Study of Conflict in American Thought, 1865–1901* (Ann Arbor, 1956). Ray Ginger's *Altgeld's America: The Lincoln Ideals Versus Changing Realities* (Chicago, 1958) is good on Chicago, and Arthur Mann's *Yankee Reformers in the Urban Age* (Cambridge, Mass., 1954) is useful for Boston. Howard H. Quint, *The Forging of American Socialism: Origins of the Modern Movement* (Columbia, S. C., 1953), covers more ground than the title indicates. Hans B. Thorelli is competent on the late nineteenth-century roots of *The Federal Antitrust Policy: Organization of an American Tradition* (Baltimore, 1955).

Three volumes in the New American Nation series contain the most up-to-date facts and interpretations of the Progressive era: Harold U. Faulkner, *Politics, Reform and Expansion,* 1890–1900 (New York, 1959); George E. Mowry, *The Era of Theodore Roosevelt, 1900–1912* (New York, 1958); Arthur S. Link, *Woodrow Wilson and the Progressive Era, 1910–1917* (New York, 1954). But it would be a mistake to overlook the older, still very useful Benjamin P. De Witt, *The Progressive Movement* (New York, 1915). For an interpretation that comes close to denying the existence of a distinct Progressive era, see Samuel P. Hays, *The Response to Industrialism, 1885–1914* (Chicago, 1957). The books by Hays, Faulkner, Mowry, and Link contain bibliographies for even the minutest problems of the subject.

The varied groups that took part in the Progressive movement are the subject of several books. For the role of businessmen, see Robert H. Wiebe, *Businessmen and Reform: A Study of the Progressive Movement* (Cambridge, Mass., 1962), and the equally sympathetic volume, John A. Garraty, *Right-Hand Man: the Life of George N. Perkins* (New York, 1960). On the elite background of the members of the Progressive party, see Alfred D. Chandler, Jr.'s very important statistical study, "The Origins of Progressive Leadership," in Elting E. Morison, ed., *The Letters of Theodore Roosevelt* (Cambridge, Mass., 1954), vol. VIII, 1462–1465. Progressive journalists are competently handled in C. C. Regier, *The Era of the Muckraker* (Chapel Hill, N. C., 1932), and with greater gusto by Louis Filler in *Crusaders for American Liberalism* (Yellow Springs, Ohio, 1950). Robert H. Bremner, *From the Depths: The Discovery of Poverty in the United States* (New York, 1956), deals expertly with social workers. The movement of Protestant clergymen to the left is the theme of Charles H. Hopkins's encyclopedic *The Rise of the Social Gospel in American Protestantism, 1860–1915* (New Haven, 1940) and of Henry F. May's more interpretive *Protestant Churches and Industrial America* (New York, 1949).

As for political leaders, Matthew M. Jo-sephson has written a sprightly, opinionated survey in *The President Makers* (New York, 1940). Those who are interested in Woodrow Wilson are urged to read and select titles from Richard L. Watson, Jr., "Woodrow Wilson and His Interpreters, 1947–1957," *Mississippi Valley Historical Review,* LXIV (September 1957), 207–236. Henry F. Pringle's *Theodore Roosevelt* (New York, 1931) is still the most readable biography of TR, but it is challenged by John M. Blum's more appreciative *The Republican Roosevelt* (Cambridge, Mass., 1954), which in turn is challenged by William H. Harbaugh's *Power and Responsibility: The Life and Times of Theodore Roosevelt* (New York, 1961). Contrast Paxton Hibben's debunking book, *The Peerless Leader, William Jennings Bryan* (New York, 1929), with Paul Glad's defense of the Great Commoner in *The Trumpet Soundeth* (Lincoln, Nebr., 1960). For the image that two political leaders had of themselves, see *La Follette's Autobiography* (Madison, Wis., 1913) and Theodore Roosevelt, *An Autobiography* (New York, 1913).

The outstanding primary sources for the New Nationalism are Herbert Croly, *The Promise of American Life* (New York, 1909); Walter E. Weyl, *The New Democracy* (New York, 1912); Walter Lippmann, *A Preface to Politics* (New York, 1914) and *Drift and Mastery* (New York, 1914). These books and the men who wrote them are the subject of a sympathetic yet severely critical study by Charles Forcey, *The Crossroads of Liberalism* (New York, 1961). For the philosophy that lay behind the New Freedom, the following are essential: Woodrow Wilson's book by that title (New York, 1913); Charles R. Van Hise, *Concentration and Control* (New York, 1912); and Louis D. Brandeis, *Other People's Money And How the Bankers Use It* (New York, 1914). William Diamond, in *The Economic Thought of Woodrow Wilson* (Baltimore, 1943), is as critical of the New Freedom as Forcey is of the New Nationalism.

Henry Steele Commager, *The American Mind* (New Haven, 1950), is practically alone today in the Parringtonian approach to the intellectual side of the Progressive movement. Some writers—among them Daniel Aaron, *Men of Good Hope* (New York, 1951); Arthur A. Ekirch, Jr., *The Decline of American Liberalism* (New York, 1955); and Louis Hartz, *The Liberal Tradition in America* (New York, 1955)—have objected, but for different reasons, to classifying Progressive thinkers as authentic reformers. At the other extreme, David W. Noble, in *The Paradox of Progressive Thought* (Minneapolis, 1958), regards the Progressives as all too typical of the liberal reform mind and dismisses them as fuzzy-minded utopians. More sympathetic are Eric F. Goldman, *Rendezvous With Destiny* (New York, 1952) and Morton G. White, *Social Thought in America* (New York, 1949), who nevertheless find fault with Progressive thinkers for being moral relativists. Richard Hofstadter, on the other hand, censures the Progressive mind for moral absolutism in the previously cited *Age of Reform.* For a novel approach to the intellectual history of the Progressive era, one that emphasizes a split between generations, see Henry F. May, *The End to American Innocence* (New York, 1959).

The local and regional variations, as well as similarities, of the Progressive movement can be found in *The Autobiography of Lincoln Steffens* (New York, 1931), an American classic by a muckraker whose investigations led him to a variety of cities and states. Two previously mentioned works, Woodward's *The Origins of the New South* and Nye's *Midwestern Progressive Politics,* make one hope that other regions will receive the attention they deserve. Winston A. Flint's *The Progressive Movement in Vermont* (Washington, D.C., 1941) is pedestrian in comparison to Ransome E. Noble, Jr.'s *New Jersey Progressivism before Wilson* (Princeton, 1946). Walton Bean's *Boss Reuf's San Francisco* (Berkeley, 1952) is a splendid companion piece to Mowry's previously cited *The California Progressives.* Contrast Robert S. Maxwell, *La Follette and the Rise of the Progressives in Wisconsin* (Madison, Wis., 1956), with William D. Miller, *Memphis during the Progressive Era, 1900–1917* (Memphis, Tenn., 1957).

The character of Progressivism in the 1920s is discussed in Kenneth C. Mackay's *The Progressive Movement of 1924* (New York, 1947); Arthur Mann's *La Guardia: A Fighter Against His Times, 1882–1933* (Philadelphia, 1959); Hofstadter's *Age of Reform;* and Goldman's *Rendezvous with Destiny.* For further reading on the 'twenties, see the bibliographical essay in Leuchtenburg's *The Perils of Prosperity.*